Amber Waves and Undertow

Amber Waves and Undertow

Peril, Hope, Sweat, and Downright Nonchalance in Dry Wheat Country

STEVE TURNER

UNIVERSITY OF OKLAHOMA PRESS : NORMAN

Library of Congress Cataloging-in-Publication Data

Turner, Steve
    Amber waves and undertow : peril, hope, sweat, and downright
nonchalance in dry wheat country / Steve Turner.
        p. cm.
    Includes bibliographical references.
    ISBN 978-0-8061-4005-6 (pbk. : alk. paper)   1. Adams County (Wash.)—
Social life and customs.   2. Farm life—Washington (State)—Adams
County.   3. Adams County (Wash.)—Rural conditions.   4. Social change—
Washington (State)—Adams County.   5. Farmers—Washington (State)—
Adams County—Biography.   6. Adams County (Wash.)—Biography.
7. Pioneers—Washington (State)—Adams County—Biography.   8. Frontier
and pioneer life—Washington (State)—Adams County.   9. Adams County
(Wash.)—Description and travel.   10. Turner, Steve, 1937- .—Travel—
Washington (State)—Adams County. I. Title.
    F897.A2T87   2009
    979.7'34—dc22
                                                                    2008032876
Maps of Adams County and the Columbia Basin copyright © 2009 by
Diane Sylvain

Cover photograph copyright © 2009 by Lionel J-M Delevingne

Copyright © 2009 by Steve Turner. Published by the University of
Oklahoma Press, Norman, Publishing Division of the University.
Manufactured in the U.S.A.

1 2 3 4 5 6 7 8 9 10

For Anne, whose loving support and encouragement made this book possible

Contents

Acknowledgments

This book owes a great deal to the literary guidance of Carol Staudacher, editor par excellence, fine writer, lasting friend. In addition, suggestions throughout by Anne Turner, and in some chapters by Susan Heinlein, Pamela Tweedy, Allison Turner, and especially corrections to chapter 10 by Mary Eleanor Bender helped to refine the manuscript. Copyeditor Jay Fultz expertly honed the text. And I am grateful indeed to editor Matt Bokovoy, who believed in this book and saw it through to publication by the University of Oklahoma Press.

I had the good fortune to meet a number of Adams County residents who became friends as well as interviewees: Donnie and, in memoriam, Norm Rambow; Grant and Nancy Miller; Roger and Blowtorch Annie Smart; Carol and Jim Kelly; Jennifer and Brent Larsen; Barry Boyer; Chris Clutter; and raconteur Roger Krug, complete with pig costume.

And Melinda Kiel and Richard Grams, who saved my life.

Many others freely gave of their time and information for my research:

Wheat Farming: in addition to the Miller and Smart families: Steve and Karen Potts, and Alma Ferderer; Ruben and Pat Fode; Gretchen Borck of the Washington Association of Wheat

Growers; Chris Holt of the U.S. Department of Agriculture; Dr. Bill Schillinger at the Dryland Research Station; and in memoriam Gene Heinemann, Bob Phillips.

Potatoes: in addition to Roger Krug: growers Frank Martinez and Mike Miller; and Dale Lathim of the Potato Growers of Washington.

Cattle Ranching: Jake Harder and, for the side trip to Mars, Maureen Harder and Mikki Kison.

Ritzville: in addition to the Rambows, Barry Boyer, Chris Clutter, and Jennifer Larsen: District Attorney Randy Flyckt, Terri Cody, Ann Hennings, Terry Janzen, Linda Kubik, Audrey Schiable, Sally Powers, John Rankin, and Sandra Fitch and her very helpful staff at the Ritzville Carnegie Library.

Lind and the Demolition Derby: in addition to Carol and Jim Kelly: Myra Horton, Bill Loomis, Esther Ware, Leroy Watson. And the Derby warriors: Frank Bren, Mike Doyle, Josh Knodel, Dawn Lobe, Amy, Grant, Karlee and Matt Miller, Chris Olson, Mark Schoesler, Gerry Schuler, Dennis Starring, Josh Wills.

Paha: Wesley and Joan Plager, John Timm, Pat Brison, LaVerne Kautz, Irma Gfeller, and in memoriam, Floyd Gleich.

Othello: Ehman Sheldon, City Administrator; Roger Krug; Olivia Vela.

Hispanic Immigration: Jeannie Enriquez, Frank Martinez, Al and Diane Ochoa, Frank Ochoa, Ehman Sheldon, Bonnie Thomas, Olivia Vela.

Anabaptist Immigration and Life: Mary Eleanor Bender; Eldress Barbara Gross of the Warden Hutterian Brethren; Pastor Terry Rediger of Menno Mennonite Church; John Stahl, Farm Boss at Stahl Hutterian Brethren.

Water: Paul Stoker, Executive Director, Columbia Basin Groundwater Management Area; Peter H. Gleick, Pacific Institute for Studies in Development, Environment, and Security.

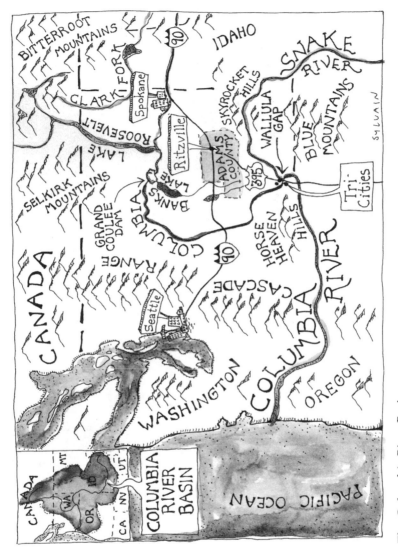

The Columbia River Basin

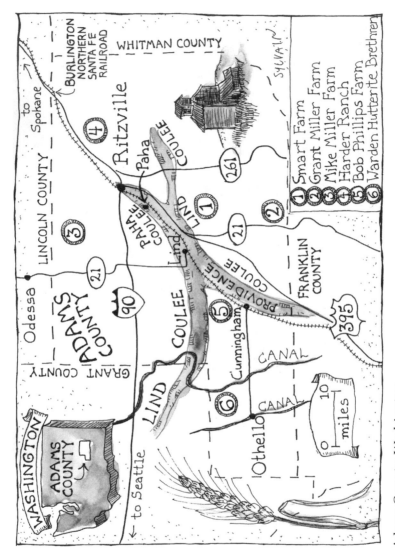

Adams County, Washington

Amber Waves and Undertow

Prelude: Noah's Gift

Setting out to see with a retrospective eye, I took the Lind-Hatton road, the two-lane blacktop that connects those towns in eastern Washington. They're fifteen miles apart in Adams County, with only an occasional human presence in between. Years before, I had claimed this road secretly as my own, so intimately did it expose the landscape, and so cleverly. The pavement is laid as though from a spool, dipping, rolling and twisting on the sagebrush terrain, never plowing its way straight or level. Mainly it tracks along the east slope of an impressive, half-mile-wide prehistoric ditch called the Providence Coulee.

In one season back then, I hauled wheat along this road to a grain elevator at a midway point called Beatrice—Bee-AA-triss—set beside the railroad that also follows the coulee. That was seed wheat—the rancher I worked for called it "birdseed"—grown thick in watered fields set (I seemed to recall) in the coulee bottom. I wanted to find that place again, to refresh my memory of combine harvester machines dancing—self-propelled, big front-end lawnmowers, jittering as they roared and bounced across the tightly packed rows. I wanted to recapture the prideful sense of being specially sent from among the crew with my truck to this place many miles away from the home ranch to haul to a special elevator.

When I reached the site where I thought that farm had been, though, there were only cattle grazing. No wheat stubble, nothing to refurbish my bright, hot recollection of those big red bouncing machines and the grain sluicing, hissing down from their projecting spouts into my truck. I got out into the great breezy silence that sits on so much of Adams County, realizing that my harvest work here was simply lost in the larger flow of change.

In this Big Bend country, time has found impressive ways to show its teeth: ice age floods, enormous almost beyond measure, shaped and reshaped the land. Plagues decimated the native peoples, and military conquest confined them to reservations. Then pioneer settlers converted what had been hunter-gatherer territory to seemingly stable agriculture.

Seemingly is the operative word. Even though time locally may appear slowed to a stop, in fact nothing here stays the same. Change may come abruptly or almost imperceptibly, but it comes. In super-slow motion, for instance, the land itself is moving away—gradually, blowing in the wind, or trickling elsewhere in the snowmelt's runoff. Underground water, too, is disappearing: pump-irrigated crop fields that border the western edge of the vast dryland wheatfields are depleting the subsurface aquifers. And in a much more evident way, forces of modern "progress" are interacting to erode the rural social fabric so basic to the national self-image—if only as mythology. Continual technological advance has led to larger farms with fewer farm families, and thus less trade for local merchants. Latter-day governmental land conservation programs have deepened that impact, further cutting into demand for farming supplies and equipment. And the onset of high-speed roads has drained away hometown retail sales to regional big-box-store malls. A slow downward trend of amenities confronts the wheat farmers, potato growers, and cattle ranchers who operate in what was already a very challenging piece of the national geography.

The moniker *Big Bend* reflects what the storied Columbia River does here. Running down from Canada in a cold, fulsome stream, it crosses into Washington and turns west not far from Spokane. Then it heads south again along the foothills of the Cascade mountain range, until it tucks back east to accept the Snake River at Pasco near the Washington/Oregon border—in effect forming a vast *C,* or, voila, a truly big bend. Then it's west again, through the spectacular Columbia Gorge, and on out to the sea.

The Bend's outcurve encloses a stack of presidential counties—Lincoln to the north, above Grant and Adams, with Garfield nearby and the revolutionary hero Franklin southernmost. And within these counties lies a primordial topography, the channeled scablands: a network of coulees (channels) up to a mile wide and five hundred feet down, gouged into the deep volcanic basalt rock of the west-sloping Columbia Plateau, gorges that twist through humped deposits and wide slopes of loess soil that rise above their banks. The term *scab* came into play because the sidewalls and the thinly covered bottoms of these coulees exposed surfaces of obviously tremendous wounds to the land. The loess that crowns away above the rock walls—a combination of silts, clays, and pulverized basalt—is so rich it will grow anything, if you give it water.

But the heavenly powers don't do that. The Cascade Range takes big helpings of the moisture coming in on prevailing westerly winds from the Pacific. The backside lands abutting these mountains are deprived: they lie in the lyrically named rain shadow, which fades only as the land slopes up slowly to the east.

By the time that rise reaches Whitman County, bordering Idaho, rainfall is sufficient for annual farming. But Adams County's rain shadow climate ranges from high desert to shrub steppe, with average precipitation (predominantly winter snow) ranging from three to twelve inches per year. The local botany shows the effects. There are no naturally grown trees, except around the few creeks and fewer spring-fed ponds and lakes. Instead, the eye finds olive shades of sagebrush and thistles, and seasonally green grasses that parch brown in high summer.

Ironically, this land once did have water—far too much, in fact. It came from the east. During the last ice age, in the Pleistocene era some 12,000 years ago, a finger of the thick Cordilleran ice sheet poked south near the Idaho border, blocking the Clark Fork's westward flow to join the Columbia. The drainage from a vast spread of mountains and valleys backed up behind this dam to form Glacial Lake Missoula, stretching eastward far into Montana, as deep as 2,000 feet, holding as much water as Lakes Erie and Ontario combined.

And then . . .

When the ice dam gave way, a flood of truly biblical proportions broke through.

A 700-foot-high slurry wall of water, mud, ice, and rock blasted out, and behind it came the entire lake. At speeds up to sixty miles per hour, the unimaginably powerful deluge gouged the coulees out of the volcanic basalts of the west-sloping Columbia Plateau and their covering of primordial soils. Early camels and other foraging creatures heard the roaring approach and felt its pressure wave well before the fatal flood arrived. But where do you go, how escape, when you can't fly? The lucky ones got to the few areas of high ground that the torrents didn't overtop.

After 150 miles of branching, rampaging destruction, the

southerly racing waters hit the Horse Heaven Hills and high ground along the Snake River, converging near today's tri-cities of Pasco, Kennewick, and Richland. Blocked by the rising hills, the torrents pooled angrily into the spreading, eventually vast but temporary Lake Lewis, where sediments carried downstream began to settle out. As pressure built, the flow of the mighty Snake reversed for some one hundred miles. Big stretches of the Walla Walla and Yakima rivers became lakes from their mouths backward. The only escape for the trapped flood was the rapidly eroding V of Wallula Gap, through which immensities of unstoppable water surged to reshape the Columbia's course to the sea. Downstream rushed ten times the combined flow of all rivers on the globe today, sixty times the volume of world's largest Amazon, power that deepened and broadened the Columbia Gorge right through the Cascades. The flood crest reaching today's Portland topped 400 feet, higher than any office tower now there. The northerly flow of the Willamette River was reversed. Boulders floating on icebergs, so-called erratics, were carried to the Pacific's shore. And the roiling outflow from the Columbia's mouth dug a trench full of flood deposits on the ocean floor, a parting gouge that curved all the way to the north coast of California.

All of this in three to four days, possibly a week of mayhem. Then, silence: the convalescent stillness of dripping and drainage, as the land began its recovery. Surviving animals coped or expired on the uphill remnants of vegetation left to them. In the vast, receding ponds of Lake Lewis and the spread-out lower reaches of the Snake, the Walla Walla, the Yakima and Palouse rivers, silts ground fine by glaciers and scoured all the way from Montana settled into mud, which dried into rich, loosely bound soils.

As eons passed, the whole scenario repeated itself again, and again, forty times or more over the two millennia during which the ice sheets shrank and advanced. And after each episode, prevailing southwesterly winds picked up the light, mineral-infused sediments the water had brought, and blew them east-northeast to settle elsewhere. The cumulative result was a spreading, map-sized fan of rich loess soils, sometimes hundreds of feet deep. The vast floods carried no Ark, floated no creatures except the drowned dead, but the richness of their residue metaphorically serves as Noah's gift.

The repetitive cataclysms ceased only when our current climate emerged some 12,000 years ago. Which is roughly when the first humans appeared in the area, and a somewhat surprising reverence for this tormented place began. These earliest inhabitants, probably migrants from Siberia who'd crossed the land bridge exposed by ice age glaciers' impoundment of ocean water, found a wealth of game, including species described by Professor Ian M. Lange, of the University of Montana, as "The Big, the Hairy, and the Bizarre"—woolly mammoths, huge bison, ground sloths, and antelope. These were dinner targets also for a nightmare assortment of saber-toothed cats, dire wolves, and short-faced bears. But the intruding humans took a greater toll, hunting the larger prey into scarcity or extinction. In consequence, their Amerind descendants had fewer game animals to choose among (and mercifully fewer too of the fearsome predators), but there still was a plenitude of antelope, deer, and rabbits. These early immigrant descendants also found major dietary addition in the rivers—salmon, especially—and filled an effective diet with nutritious native plants.

To the Palouse, the Wallawalla, the Cayuse, and the Nez Perce, this was home ground, where they found their physical and spiritual sustenance. The spring blossoms that so avidly punctuate the severe landscape—yellow of rabbit brush and sage, orange of hawkweed, and purple of larkspur—include the blue of camas and white of bitterroot that guided native gatherers to the edible roots below.

Pressed by the U.S. Army to sell tribal lands to settlers, the Nez Perce's famed Chief Joseph replied that the earth is "too sacred to be valued by or sold for silver or gold. . . . The Creative Power, when he made the earth, made no marks, no lines of division or separation on it. . . . We love the land; it is our home. We will not sell the land. We will not give up the land."[1]

And they did not willingly do so. In retrospect, there was never any outcome possible other than violence and domination as an unending flow of immigrants pressured the natives to make room for new and different uses of their homeground, and the natives resisted. What doubt existed on either side as to the eventual end result was forcefully put to rest by the U.S. Army.

The Cayuse war of 1848–50 drove all Indians out of the Walla Walla Valley, onto reservations. The Yakima war of 1855–58 did the same for the tribes in the Big Bend. The Palouse and the Nez Perce, particularly, were moved away from their homelands, superior acreage that the settlers especially wanted. But there was one last spasm of resistance to come. In 1877 Chief Joseph led the Nez Perce and allied reservation inmates in a heroic attempt to gain independence in Canada. Along the way, the freedom-seeking Indians encountered truly premonitory evidence of what lay ahead: early tourists who'd come to see the wonders of what is now Yellowstone National Park. But the army pursued and caught up with Joseph's band, and the bloody result was the return of the survivors to reservation captivity.

So the original residents of the Big Bend were removed, the land cleared for newcomers' settlement. Protective military forts were built near the trading posts at Walla Walla and Colville, and filled with the menace of troops. A new order came over the land.

The ethos of Manifest Destiny instructed that era's public

opinion on the matter of who had what rights to the land. So the injustice of such forcible transfer was written off—by the winners—to racial superiority and an ostensibly God-given higher purpose: to farm.

The change in ethnic control, though, did not alter the basic fact of human dependence on the land. The natives in their sparse numbers had learned to take what the land offered. The newcomers wanted to make it offer more. That was not easy. Settlers in what was to become Adams County struggled to adapt their farming to the rich but arid soil, learning the hard way that only by lying fallow for a year did their fields take in enough moisture to grow a decent crop. In the process, they formed an attachment to the ground as strong in its own way as that of the natives they displaced.

"The land is a gift, and you treat it accordingly," said retired farmer Gene Heinemann. Wheat grower Grant Miller puts it more strongly. "The land is sacred. The home ranch is sacred."

And in Adams County, it's mainly grain now that gives the color of food in the inception. Potatoes also take importance in their irrigated crop circles, and cattle in the eastern scablands. But it's wheat that dominates in the vast spreads of the county's drylands. Ruben Fode, retired also from farming, says "This land has its own beauty. In the spring when the wheat is green and heading out, that's beautiful. Damn, I love that. The dirt's in my blood."

This is the story, ongoing, of this strikingly unusual place, and of the intriguing variety of people its dirt sustains: life in the rain shadow, and Adams County in particular.

1

Icons on the Home Ground

When I first saw harvest, at Bob Phillips's ranch in 1957, unsettling changes were powerfully under way in Adams County. But the propulsive forces were still being called "progress," the working out of a natural order of things that, on balance, appeared beneficent. The undertow beneath the amber waves was largely undetected—or, when foreseen, assigned to the list of things to deal with tomorrow.

On a return visit in 2004, roving around the area, I came on an abandoned farmstead out west of the Lind-Hatton Road that had preserved a microcosm, a sort of unintended museum diorama of that most compelling agent of change—mechanization. The place was close to the now disappeared settlement of Providence. Beside a back driveway near the weathered-down barn sat a row of four abandoned trucks, each successively younger, from the very early days of truckhood to perhaps the 1940s. Resting not far away was a rusting combine harvester machine of the pre-gasoline sort that originally would have been pulled by horses, half a century before the self-propelled models to come. This assemblage of antique vehicles made a kind of still life painted in reality, a collected illustration of stopped time that fascinated the eye.

The house, slightly upslope on the hilltop, was one-storey, clapboard, comfortably sized for a family. And vacant: empty for years, the weather having its way through the broken windows, the missing shingles.

You get a sense of foreboding from a place like this, as though there might be a ghostly presence inside, or echoes of things you don't want to hear. Abandoned homesteads are a fairly common sight in the Adams wheatlands, and I've visited several. Usually they're just . . . *exposed*—walk right in if you dare. In this case, an expensive steel pipe swing gate blocked the approach driveway (interested visitors like me just steered around it in the well-established wheel tracks, since the connecting fence was gone). So someone in the family still cared about it. Seems likely that by the time the parental generation retired or otherwise departed, their children were established elsewhere, but still respected the home ranch.

Others of these vacancies, however, are simply evidence of farmers who didn't make it, whose lands were taken over by their more successful neighbors. That's the prevalent pattern here, unlike other cropland areas around the country where the shrinkage in active farm-owning families is the flip side of corporatized agriculture.

I have a poignant memory of the first orphaned homestead I saw, one day during the Phillips harvest. After the combines had mowed the opening swath around a ripe, hilly field, I took my truck up to a ridgetop to wait for the next off-loading they would need. Cresting the rise, I found a small farmhouse, five rooms at the most, cinched tight within the surrounding wheat. All glass in the few windows was gone. Harsh sun had turned the clapboard siding deep brown.

The wide, multi-row seed planting drill had swept as close to the dwelling as it could go, fore and aft, leaving the structure sitting like a pupil in a bare open Egyptian eye amidst the grain we were cutting. Wheat grew up to within six feet of the front stoop.

I wondered who had taken the last step down there. Who had hated to leave, and who had been glad to go.

Whichever way it was, they went, and so did many others. It's emblematic of a shrinking population of landholders that these houses, habitable for their founding families, had no takers once the original occupants were gone. They'd become useless structures, the acreage around them absorbed into the holdings of more successful neighbors.

The Providence Road ranch, however, was remarkable for its companion display of vehicular history. It's not unusual in Adams County to see broken-down or outmoded farm equipment abandoned, left to rust in some unplanted place: worn-out disc harrows and seed drills with weeds growing through them, ancient harvester machines tucked up in small dry coulees to wait out eternity. What else to do with tons of useless machinery, out here so far from any scrap metal dealer who would cut it up to recycle?

But retired trucks are not the norm among such discards. These motorized workhorses tend to get traded or sold rather than dumped. Roofers, particularly, are fond of retired grain trucks: the hoist backs are perfect for carrying loads of old shingles to the landfill. But that's only one example. Generally speaking, people somewhere will wring the last miles of toil out of these faithful machines before total exhaustion takes them to junkyards.

So the lineup of old trucks so neatly parked out on that Providence Road place testified to a family's mode of thriftiness—wear it out before you replace it—as well as affection for favored equipment that transmutes into a mechanized form of pethood. But

the Providence Road display also measured a crucial development in the changes that have made modernity here what it is.

It's an obvious fact that those trucks, and the vehicles that preceded them, needed roads. And it is roads—dirt, macadam and
rail, and their precursors, the trails—that have changed this land
so completely: the roads and what they've brought, what they've
enabled, and what they've killed—right up to the present.

One could argue that the best way to preserve some sort of
purity in human communities is to isolate them. But that doesn't
happen. The flow of people and goods from one place to another
—for trade, settlement, or conquest—has been a primary component of recorded history. So also in the Big Bend. For many
hundreds of years before Europeans arrived, colored beads, flints
with durable cutting edges, and other valued goods were moving
in slow exchange from as far as South America to the native tribes
in the Columbia Basin.

The Spanish invasions of Central and South America in the
fifteenth century put new entries onto that trade route. Horses,
on the positive side. But on the negative, sickness: viruses such
as smallpox and measles, bred in Europe and Asia, new to the
native Americans. The Indians had no resistance to these foreign
microbes, and the results were devastating. By the time settlers
arrived in the late 1800s, the peoples they would evict had been
heavily depleted—although some still put up a fight.

Move the clock forward half a century, and we find trade
routes both aiding and injuring Adams County's newcomers as
well, albeit with less lethal impact. General stores that had given
outlying hamlets both character and focus were going under in
favor of larger emporiums in central towns. Onward a few more
decades, and the scope broadens: demand for a faster automotive connection between the expanding commercial centers of
Spokane to the north and the tri-cities to the south—Pasco, Ken-

newick, and Richland—caused upgrading of that stretch of U.S. Route 395 to four lanes divided, right through Adams County. That brought a painful 1957 bypassing of Lind and other Big Bend towns.

The result wasn't entirely without merit: the original two-lane stretch of this national highway that *S*-curved steeply down to Lind at the bottom of the coulee had become a sort of death alley, according to Adams County's affable development analyst, Roger Krug. "You know there's those wicked bends on that stretch of road," said Roger. "People were just flying off there and getting killed. So that's one reason they closed it. But man, that did bad things to Lind."

As one local history put it, when the bypass went in, "next morning all the professional men in town were gone."

2

The Mixed Blessing of Roads

The god of roads must resemble the Romans' two-faced Janus, one face looking forward, and one back. But the image also needs its theatrical adaptation—one face smiling, one in a frown.

The smiler is looking forward: build that road! The frown comes from considering what will happen in consequence. Of course, you have to choose up sides on both counts. Roads—and those other modes of pre-automobilic travel, river boat and rail—do bring change, and since early in the nineteenth century in the Columbia Basin, that change has meant development of one sort or another. Although it's tempting to think that the god's frown is strictly for the uprooted natives, the smile did not prove lasting for many of those who replaced them.

In fact, the question does rise as to why settlers came to Adams County at all. Ross Cox, one of the earliest non-Indians to see this land, thought it was about as awful as any place he'd ever been. He passed through in August of 1812 with a party of fur traders. His book *Adventures on the Columbia River* narrated that expedition, and he was not an admirer of what he saw:

> . . . [N]o green spot bloomed around us. The country was completely denuded of wood; and as far as the eye extended,

16

nothing was visible but immense plains covered with parched brown grass, swarming with rattlesnakes.[1]

Great promotional material! And indeed the first of the emigrant routes into the Columbia Basin skirted the drylands, heading for the lush greenness of the Willamette Valley beyond the Cascades. That was the Oregon Trail—a truly primitive wagon road, to be sure, but very effective in starting the conversion from native to settler society in eastern Washington. In 1843, a "great migration" along the trail brought almost one thousand newcomers to an area that was not yet even part of the United States. The vast northwestern spread known then only as the Oregon Country contained all of present-day Oregon, Washington, and Idaho, plus parts of Wyoming, Montana, and British Columbia west of the Rockies. Russia and Spain had sold away their interests in the place, so it was shared for exploitation exclusively by England and the United States. Not until 1846 was the current international boundary drawn with Canada, and not until 1848 did all this land (minus the British Columbia portion) become the congressionally certified Oregon Territory.

Most of the early wagoneers trudged and rafted through the excruciating portages and wild water rides of the Columbia Gorge, onward to Willamette country. But a significant northerly branch of the trail brought groups of trekkers—particularly those needing medicine or supplies—to the Whitman Mission in the Walla Walla river valley, which crosses the far eastern reach of today's Oregon-Washington border. With months of plodding progress behind them, many found this lesser destination green enough to suit—particularly when they were beguiled by the Whitmans. Marcus and Narcissa of that name were easterners who in 1836 established a mission not far from the present-day city of Walla Walla, aiming to convert the Cayuse people and other nearby natives to Christianity and an agrarian lifestyle. New York-born Narcissa apparently hated where she was, and could hardly conceal her disdain for the Cayuse, so unexcited as they were by the prospects of Christian farming. Nonetheless, she and Marcus ardently promoted settlement in their area, and beyond it, the Palouse region and the Big Bend. Trail-weary settlers began to take their advice.

Among those who lingered at the Mission to consider the prospect was a group arriving in 1847, several of them sick with the measles. Marcus, a medical doctor, did his best with the ensuing epidemic. But the Cayuse, lacking immunity to the virus, and falling like flies, decided it was his medicine that was carrying them off. Other native resentments of treatment by whites boiled up to further inflame the situation. In consequence, Narcissa, Marcus, and most of their emigrant guests were slaughtered. Only children were spared.

The military responded, and in the resulting Cayuse War, the surviving natives lost their lands. The Whitmans' revenge, as it were, materialized in the white faces and plowed fields appearing where the Indians had lived and hunted and assumed their way of life would go on forever.

With the threat of hostilities largely suppressed, attention turned to the federal government's desire to promote settlement in the West—in this case, particularly, to justify the United States' possession of the Oregon Country. Captain John Mullan and troops from Fort Walla Walla began work on a wagon route— which came to be known as the Mullan Road—from that headquarters all the way to Fort Benton in Montana, last stop for upriver steamboats on the Missouri River. As part of this new highway project, the rudimentary trailway north to the Hudson Bay Company's Fort Colville, near Spokane, was improved and transformed into the Colville Road. As described by Ruth Kirk and Carmela Alexander in their excellent *Exploring Washington's Past: A Road Guide to History*, these were brutal changes:

> Mullan's men laid corduroy [*i.e.,* logs placed side by side] across swamps, cut trees at ground level, removed obstructing rocks, and built hundreds of river crossings. . . . By 1862 wagons could lurch over the resulting swath from the western edge of the Great Plains, across the Rocky Mountains, to the pine country of Spokane and the sagebrush flats [on the eastern edge of Adams County] leading to Walla Walla.[2]

Aside from their combined military and civilian clientele, these new thoroughfares shared a kind of victor's arrogance: they gouged their way along the native peoples' traditional travelways. Indeed, for their first fifty-odd miles, the Mullan and the Colville ran together on the chiefest of those time-honored trails, the favored course between the Cayuse country and the territory of the Spokanes. This ancient route came up from the Walla Walla valley, and crossed the Snake at its confluence with the Palouse River. Fleets of native canoes there presaged 1859's Lyons Ferry toll boat and bridges the future would bring. Nearby, the trail passed the principal village of Palus, a name taken by emigrants and applied to the Sahaptian people who lived there—as also to the spreading loess lands to the north and east where they hunted, to the river, even to the tribe's prized Appaloosa horses.

So, too, the trail was taken, transmogrified into a transport corridor for the soldiers, the settlers, miners, freighters, herders. Soon, all that was left of nearly ten thousand years of native existence in the Palouse country was the name.

By the 1850s, stockmen were moving herds of horses, cattle, and sheep onto the Big Bend's dryland plains, particularly where large swaths occurred of the yard-high, nutritious Bluebunch

Wheatgrass. This otherwise unassuming botanic denizen was nicknamed the "ice cream plant" because it fattened range animals so quickly (fur trader Ross Cox's invidious description doubtless was made at high summer, when even this luscious plant would have seemed dry and unattractive.) Sheep and cattle loved it, and in consequence essentially ate it to death: it's no longer a common plant in the area.

But the more staid practice of farming was edging in, too. A harbinger showed up in an ill-fated shipping solution devised by early grain growers—a wheat loading chute perilously constructed down the banks of the deep gorge of the Snake in what is now Franklin County, Adams's southern neighbor. It was one of those inventions whose time had not come: the design required a conduit so steep that the contents of the wheat sacks dumped into it up top were scorched from friction by the time they reached the waiting vessels below.

Nonetheless, the first contingent of grain growers was expanded by a steady, if dwindling, flow of farmers along the Oregon Trail and its linked Mullan Road extension. There were rebounders, too: land-hungry sojourners who found the Willamette Valley too crowded or too expensive. After passage of the federal Homestead Act in 1862, farmers and speculators alike began to claim quarter-section sites—160 acres—particularly in the better-watered Palouse country to the east of the coulees. The process was further accelerated in 1873 when Congress adopted the Timber Culture Act, offering free proprietorship of an additional quarter to settlers who promised to plant trees, so starkly missing in the grasslands of the Big Bend.

But difficulty of access had become an issue. Not for the last time, emigrants discovered that the overland route to the acreage they had longed for was somewhat less than welcoming. Kirk and Alexander's account of the Mullan enterprise continues, describing what even the most skillful land agents could not conceal:

> Rockslides and washouts soon changed the "road" to a mule trail, however, and wheeled travel became all but impossible. Immigrants in 1865 reported that "any other method" of reaching the Northwest would surely be better than the Mullan Road.[3]

During the 1860s and '70s, river traffic responded to part of that wish. Steamboats carrying crowds of prospectors and homesteaders ran from portage to portage up the Columbia from Portland, and on along the lower Snake. But emigrants who relaxed on the water passage still had to beat their way from the river docks inland, needing roads.

Or, for part of the way, at least, railroads. By 1880, Henry Villard's Oregon Railroad & Navigation Company was laying tracks from its Columbia River landing at Wallula into the Walla Walla Valley and the lower Palouse country. And in 1881, the Northern Pacific Railroad (NPRR), soon to become a cash cornucopia for financiers James J. Hill and J. P. Morgan, built a mainline section from the Columbia docks straight through the still largely un-homesteaded dry zone to Spokane. When these linked systems were connected to Portland in 1882, the steamboats' glory days were over.

The era of boundaries and formal government had begun. By the 1880s, an array of new administrative entities, like a set of nesting boxes unpacked and pressed together, had rationalized the map of the Pacific Northwest.

In 1853, the Oregon Territory begat the lesser Washington Territory, with its eastern edge still extended to the crest of the Rocky Mountains. Year 1863 saw the Idaho Territory formed, and Wash-

ington's boundaries were set as they are today. The Washington
pre-state, in turn, begat (among others) Whitman County, containing all the better-watered, more heavily settled Palouse country, plus much of the mostly unpopulated Big Bend drylands to
the west. And in 1883, with the NPRR tracks in place, Whitman
County begat our homeground of Adams County.

Well, actually the Territorial Legislature did that begetting
(statehood did not come until 1889), but it was essentially the
northwestern quarter of Whitman that 150 very ambitious local
residents claimed for Adams. As it turned out, they had admirable
foresight. But remembering Ross Cox's description of the sere,
snake-filled landscape, in retrospect they seem . . . cockeyed. Nonetheless, Adams's founding families—Bennett, McKay, Whittlesey,
and Wells, among others—proceeded to form a government and
in 1890 set the county seat at Ritzville. The future city was named
for orchardist and land speculator Phillip Ritz, who built the first
hotel there.

The charm was the railroad. In its seventy-five diagonal miles
through Adams, the NPRR dug a number of wells, spaced out
along the line. They were there to supply the engines, of course,
but there was need also to show hopeful immigrants that underground water was available. The federal government wanted to
speed habitation in its western territories, so Congress had granted
the railroad companies large amounts of land along their proposed routes as an inducement to lay track. Accordingly, the companies badly needed settlers to buy this ground, sales thereof to
pay for construction costs and profits. The Northern Pacific's advertisements for cheap land, described in glowing and, in this case,
inaccurate terms, were published throughout Europe as well as
America's east and midwest.

Speculators such as Ritz, counting on the success of this pro-
motion, bought either railroad acreage or land nearby. Ritz ac-

quired enough for a townsite, as well as adjoining prospective farmland. As an inducement for immigrants to alight and set roots, he planted a line of sapling maples and other trees eventually parched along stretches of the rails near his intended town. It was a laughably transparent bit of camouflage, given that beyond these scrawny imports, no arboreal presence was to be seen except beside the rare seeps and creeks.

But the railroad's strategy worked. Wherever a well went down, a town grew up: Hatton, Cunningham, Providence, Lind. And between Lind and Ritzville there was Paha, where the water came up by itself in a highly unusual spring-fed flow that supplied a pond and a grove of trees. Along with these station-stop towns, though, came a problem. How were the new settlers to get back and forth to their claims through the tangle of grasses and sagebrush, and the wheel-trapping floury soil? No surprise that the most pressing business confronting Adams's new commissioners at their first meeting was the division of the county into Road Districts One and Two. Within six months, the first official roads had been created, one each westbound and northbound from the county seat, intersecting a growing network of farm lanes spreading in the back country.

The surveyors of the Big Bend country had imposed an etch-a-sketch grid of section lines, north-south, east-west, defining every square mile of the territory. One section equals 640 acres equals one square mile, the standard land measurement in all the trans-Mississippi West. In the Big Bend, only the irregularities of flood channel coulees interrupted this rigid overlay.

As these section squares began to fill in with farms, settlement centers also evolved at wagon's reach, every ten to fifteen miles or so amidst the surrounding, implanted population. There would be a school, a store, a post office, a church—Lutheran, Mennonite, or other Protestant denomination, occasionally Catholic, depending on who had congregated nearby. Some also had cemeteries. These small outposts—sometimes called post office settlements—took names from their founding families: Delight, Harriston, Mc-Call; Ralston, Schrag, Willis, many others.

The farm lanes in the outback served by these centers ran geometrically along the section boundaries, skirting everyone's property. And so the developing map of local roadways began to look —on paper—like something printed by a waffle iron. But on the ground, the result was much more that of a fishnet draped over the steeply rolling land: straight lines, but only in the sense of compass direction. Otherwise, it was all up and down. These lanes made no pretense of grading or paving—they simply lay on the land, regardless of rise or declivity. And almost every mile saw plenty of both, sometimes at breathtaking pitch.

Subsequent improvement cut through the tops of some hills, and put fill in the deeper draws. Later came thick coatings of gravel, crushed from the prevalent dark gray basalt rock (and, since 1980, also featuring the pale mixed-in residue of abrasive volcanic ash erupted by Mt. St. Helens). At speeds higher than twenty-five miles per hour, vehicles lacking four-wheel drive encounter a queasiness of steering similar to that on the thawing surfaces of cold country dirt roads in springtime before the subsurface frost departs. Even with a loaded truck, drivers ignore this dryland hydroplaning at their peril: get your wheels too close to the edge, and you may be going off. I saw that sad result on one of my haul trips to Beatrice. At the bottom of a steep draw, there was a truck down off the road on its side, the load of wheat spilled out in a thick dirtied fan. The driver, a kid from another ranch, had climbed out unhurt to sit on the now horizontal cab door, with his legs hanging down in front of the truck's exposed underparts. I slowed to shout did he need help, but he waved me off, his face disconsolate. Indeed. He had a hard evening ahead.

I got used to the mushy steering. A loaded truck pretty much forces its way through the gravel, as long as you aim straight. But empty—or in a car—if you get too eager with speed, the road can be really unsettling. So you learn to slow down.

Regardless, there's still the dust, always. Any vehicle moving on these gravel roads at traveling speed kicks up an impressive, roiling cloud that trails behind for a considerable distance (and often engulfs you when movement stops). In car or truck, one travels with rearview obscured, and with the constant whooshing white noise of tires through gravel that gives a sense of suspension, isolation, ground-level flight. Which becomes a near reality when cresting some of the rises—going up with power in the single set of mid-road tire grooves that divert to the side for safety at the last minute, lest you meet the unlikely someone coming the other way. Then feeling the slight loss of gravity in your stomach, and confidence in your head, as you release the accelerator and the vehicle plummets downward, your foot hovering over the brake pedal.

Unless you're simply focused on getting where you're going, there's an exhilaration to this traverse: seeing the land open out at the crests, cinch down in the draws, your eyes taking in first the precision, then the blur of colors and textures, crops, wild grasses, sagebrush, scab coulee. Your truck, or your car, in this mode an extension of yourself, feeling and enjoying the landforms almost as if rolling with pleasure over the frontal amenities of a Renoir nude.

I'd like to think there may have been some of that sense, or whatever version of it was prevalent then, for drivers in the days when these lanes were first opened. But I doubt it. Travel was too difficult, too slow. Originally, my graveled backroads were dirt, compacted in ruts by the wheels of the farm wagons—which had no easy time in their first episodes of passage, because the soils are so fine-grained and deep. Draft animals tired miserably with the pulling. The restrained forward pace gave no escape from the cloud of dirt-dust stirred up by hooves and wheels. When fall rains came, farmers had to spread straw in the ruts to firm up mud that mired their rigs. My whooshing white noise back then was the jingle and creak of harness, the groaning of wagon flex, screeching of brake levers, shouted commands of drivers, grunting and panting of the animals, the stirred-up earth invading the eyes, the nose and mouth with its stale, tan smell, its sour-tasting grit. My vehicle's power up the hill was the straining of mules or horses, eyes futile behind blinders, chests heaving, mouths perhaps foaming with effort, the rank, warm odor of their sweat and muscle blending with the brown floating, all-coating flour of the dust. And on the downslopes, think of it: legs trembling to hold back the weight, the animals' amazingly trim fetlocks and cannon bones planting the hooves to sink just deep enough to find firmness, and avoid disaster.

But many of the settlers' new small-town centers did not have the same holding power. Roads to the larger townsites took names from their destinations: Marcellus Road, Ralston Road, Cunningham Road, Lind-Hatton. Meanwhile, the section-edging lanes began to sort out winners and losers, taking the names of families that prospered: Kulm, Phillips, Harder, for instance, intersecting across the landscape. One can trace county history in this network of designations—as also in the choices of which routes from harvest to market, to shipping points, would get official attention. The resources of the county and the state had to focus on some of these potentials, to the exclusion of others. So began the selective process that had such higher-level impact in Rte. 395's bypassing of Lind. And as the twentieth century opened, these choices increasingly tied themselves to the burgeoning culture of the automobile.

Today's syndrome of small-town commerce plowed down by regional big box merchandisers had its precursor in earlier decades. The offerings at stores in the dispersed small-town centers had been meager. By the 1930s, successful farmers had adopted automobiles and trucks as well as tractors. Pressure for road improvements kept pace, making distance travel easier. People began seeking better deals farther away. The Ritzville Trading Company, for instance, a department store almost before that term was definitive, became the largest such emporium in the Big Bend.

In consequence, the tiny town centers . . . disappeared. All of the post offices mentioned above, and many more, gone. Even towns founded in faith, such as Menno, center for Mennonite worshippers, evaporated. The church there survived, and continues active, but not the town. As a measure of that change, faithful Menno congregants now drive as much as twenty miles to attend services.

As it happens, the main two-lane road that brings them to church has been for years paved and well maintained, albeit very like the profile of a sine wave. With modern cars and infrequent traffic, twenty miles on this road means twenty minutes or just a few more (on the old roads, a church-bound horse and buggy might make six miles per hour, a Model-T Ford perhaps fifteen).

Just so, the vastly increased competence of automobiles, the allure of speed, and the quality of pavement help to obscure the social cost of rural freeways. Want to drive from the isolation of Lind to the retail refulgence of Moses Lake, with its Wal-Mart, Staples, Kmart, Safeway, and other big emporiums? Less than an hour of air-conditioned, surround-sound comfort via nicely graded Rte. 395 and east-west Interstate 90. To the movies and concerts and big stores in Spokane? An hour. Big highways in rural territory offer the seduction of clock-defeating speed to regional cornucopias as balm for the damage they've done.

No surprise, then, that the people who mourn the decline of Lind and other bypass-bitten towns nonetheless enjoy the highway that helped bring their municipal miseries. So do I, because four-lane, divided Rte. 395 is one of the most beautiful roads in the region. It's a road of arousal, especially in the stretch between Lind and Ritzville—plying to the sensuousness of the land it traverses, and offering that to the driver. It rims the lip of the deep Paha Coulee, one of the lesser flow channels carved by the ice age floods. But "lesser" in this context still means vast. One-hundred-fifty feet down, half a mile across. All measures of landscape in this territory are . . . *big*.

And in their muted way, expressive. In spring, the wheatfields mounding above the coulee's edge show dark-lawn green, or un-planted fallow tan. The gouged-out coulee, with soils skimpy on its sides but fertile in the bottom, offers green then too—but it's the lighter tones of wild grasses and weeds, interspersed by sagebrush. And there are flowers, blue swaths of forget-me-nots, purple camas, orange hawkweed.

By late summer, early fall, the harvested fields display tawny bristle rows of stubble. Winter will bring screes of snow to make abstract patterns of this stippled cropland. But in the autumn coulee, only the dusty sage and rabbitbrush have any verdure: the flowers are gone, and the grasses and weeds have turned dry brown. The resulting, all-pervading dun coloration is so seamless and ordinary that the eye denies the vast scope of the Paha's trough—until you notice that the Burlington-Northern train running along its bottom looks Disney-sized.

There's no fear of falling from 395, however. It cooperates comfortably with the subtly folded backslope between the coulee's descent and the wheatfields above. The road is so confident of its intimacy with the contours of the wide, uphill cusp that its north and southbound sections flex separately, sometimes even losing sight of each other. And while the southbound roadway is a smooth, dark asphalt composite, the northbound lanes are tanned white concrete, a surface that makes your tires sing slightly at 70 mph, the state's gracious speed limit through the slow rise and fall, the long, slightly banked curves of this freeway, so well fitted to the surface that the enraptured car feels tuned to the turning of the earth: seems to be standing still as the land passes beneath.

Sadly, enjoying the road helps to shield the fact that the centralizing commercial economy it supports is sucking the life out of the small towns that gave rise to a national ethos: towns whose communal values are still claimed as bedrock of the American psyche even as their reasons for existence are wiped out. It's ironic also that the costly erosive impact of roads such as 395 on municipalities along its corridor is routinely flipped to positive on the balance sheet of disinterested *progress*. Macroeconomists measure this deterioration at the small scale as just the necessity of adapting those towns, or what's left of them, to an evolving national economy that finds no profit in the pride of residential history—that coldly pulls up the roots of its origins as it consolidates and rewards only efficiency.

Yet the freeways charting this new age can't leave all history behind: they have to acknowledge significant crossroads, routes named for municipal destinations, even though those towns have withered or vanished. Accordingly, there are intersections on the Adams stretch of Interstate 90 marked for Schrag and Tokio, sites now only of grain elevators. And both I-90 and Rte. 395 honor the Paha-Packard Road with exits, a route named a century ago when both locations were actual settlements. Now Paha has two non-historic homes, some relict, disintegrating houses, and an aging pair of elevators. Packard, sixteen miles north, is evident only as a modernized grain storage silo. Yet because of the route's name, these nonexistent places are still enshrined on the map.

So that road has its own life—a well maintained, two-lane hard surface local route to Odessa and other Lincoln County towns to the north. And if you take the Paha-Packard exit from 395, dipping down into the coulee and winding up the other side, you find at the crest the more compelling way that Paha and other expiring villages silently left their mark: their burial grounds, their dead.

Inside a negligible wire fence, Paha's cemetery crowns a hilltop that shows a view for miles all around. Many miles, the land rolling in its humps and vales. Latter-day farmsteads, widely spaced, headquarters now of cropland spreads acquired from those whose earlier efforts failed, float within their green windbreak containments on the variegated sea of wheat, fallow ground, and stretches of wild grasses punctuated by sagebrush.

There's a small, identifying signpost, one of those that the state puts up for every cemetery, but when I first went there the ground it demarcates had gone to tenacious weeds, hip high, wide-fronded mustard most prominent among them. Only one family gravesite—that of the Plagers—was kept clear, decorated with plastic flowers. Inside its low stone outline one finds a spired monument to *Pauline, wife of G. Plager, 7/3/1855–8/7/1907. "She was the sunshine of our life."* Other markers commemorate *Ruby*, born and died in 11/1917, *Mary A., 1886–1910*, and, simply, *Mother* and *Father*.

Elsewhere, headstones are scattered at random in the bracken. The dispersed plots surely were bought with the expectation that the cemetery would fill up, but it did not. The unused distances between graves tell of how the town's death came to rest here along with those few who lie in the earth. Though abandoned, let them not be forgotten: *Lewis Jones, 1840–1912, wife Mary*

1854–1898. Mother Elizabeth, wife of Peter Poston 2/15/1874–3/17/1917. J.S.S. Rouse 12/3/1844–10/5/1897. In loving memory of wife and mother Helen Roe, wife of W. F. Newland, 11/4/1846–12/23/1894. Geo. C. Osborn, died 4/24/1896, aged 31 yrs, 6 ms, 11ds. Bessie Gregg, June 1891–January 1892. Strouse, Aaron 1847–1915, Mary his wife 1845–1932. Willie Sweeney, son of W & Sarah Sweeney, born 7/13/1900, died 10/21/1905, age 5 yrs 3 mos 8 days. Emma A. Johnson, At Rest, 5/13/1874–1/7/1926, Charles Johnson 1875–1938.

And here is where I find Salena E. Savage, dead in 1890 at age seventeen, and left behind—the only one of that surname identified in the graveyard. *Our precious one hath gone before, to greet us on the blissful shore.* Her marker of white marble calls to the eye, alone out near one edge of this forlorn, square place. It is late summer, the mustard leafless and dried brown—a crackling, brittle, leg-impeding jungle. Mindful of the badger holes and possible rattlesnakes, I forge a path, the sharp, brown smell and dust of the disturbed dry weeds rising around me.

The stone is graceful, almost preternaturally clean. The nicely engraved flower below the arched top testifies to her family's sense of special loss. Except for the obelisk and carefully made stones in the Plager family plot, most other markers in this burial ground are stark in their lack of decoration, some almost rudimentary.

There are days when rain and wind lash this promontory, when snow falls. But this day offers only a light, occasional breeze under a vast blue sky. And the stillness, the distance all around, gathers a contemplation. I think of the lovely concept in Thornton Wilder's *Our Town*, in which the dead talk with each other from grave to grave. I hope they do that here, because otherwise it is so entirely lonely.

I clear space in front of Salena's stone: the mustard stems snap easily, the spray of fronds at their tops acting as partial parachutes as I toss the plants away. I talk to her for a while, telling her how different the world is now, vowing to come back from time to time. I get no sense of response, but my own sentiments create the ambience of connection. As I rest quietly, looking out over the surrounding miles of land, my mind brings me strains of Debussy's *Maid with the Golden Hair.* It seems a fitting requiem for this moment.

Far across, below the other lip of the coulee, miniature, inaudible trucks and cars move along on 395, their speed dampered to dreamlike slowness by the distance. Their presence, seen from the vantage point of these past lives, this interment of history, is insignificant.

The cemetery is not visible from the four lanes of 395. But the sere, spare gravity of this burial ground stays with me when I reenter the big road. At first I drive slowly, fearful of breaking the connection. As the planing highway gives me back the timeless flow of the land, though, my gathering speed, undertoned by the singing tires, makes a warp in which Salena's resting place travels with me. One can heedlessly drive by, or even through, such abandoned places and simply log them as casualties of mindless developmental forces. But that's not all they were. And I had stopped long enough for the ghost of Paha to work its way past such an easy categorization: it had become impossible to ignore, let alone forget.

As I was to learn, this town did not fail without giving color to the past.

3

Up and Down:
Two Families, One Town

We first encounter Allen Jeremiah and Mary Ann (George) Savage struggling through the noisy dockside turmoil of Liverpool, England, in 1871. They are burdened with luggage, and Mary Ann carries their two-year-old son William. Married three years, they're bound for a new life in America—and going the hard way: across the stormy North Atlantic in the crowded, seasick-smelling steerage deck of a side-wheel packet steamer. Mary Ann is nearing the end of her second trimester with James Henry, so in retrospect one wishes especially for her no storms during that often awful passage.

They survived that trip and embarked on another, across land this time, settling on a farm in Illinois. Twice more they moved to other farms there while five more children arrived: Salena, Cora Belle, Levi, Martha, and lastly Allen Jr., born in 1883.

Five years later, the lure of western acreage and the Northern Pacific's blandishments drew them to emigrate again. They traveled once more at the lowest level of amenity, packed with their goods in a stifling emigrant car—basically a compartmented moving van with windows, offering a trip not unlike steerage in a steamship but without the sickening heave and roll. After perhaps a week on the rails, they reached Adams's brand new county seat, Ritzville. At the land office, Allen and Mary Ann chose acreage to the south as their destination. Equipped with a wagon and team of horses, they set out with their children to homestead a quarter-section of intended wheatland in the uphill, rolling terrain a mile west of the depot at Paha.

At the time, this town existed mainly in the Northern Pacific's imagination, expressed as a plat of a village with two streets paralleling the tracks. A railroad section gang was barracked there. And a post office had been established in Lem Jones's newly opened general store, one of those crucial frontier establishments where settlers could order fence wire, and buy everything from harness and nails and tools to canned goods, flour, and sugar.

The other significant feature of the town-to-be was its plentiful water supply, so deep its location was in the coulee bottom. Wells there along the new streets found water not very far down. And the surface flow from the spring ponded so nicely amidst the shading grove of trees.

It was dry uphill, though, where a cemetery had been dedicated as part of the town plan. And there the Savage family made an even stronger connection with the ground than their homestead. The town's second burial was Salena Elizabeth, dead of tuberculosis in 1890. She was seventeen. *Our precious one hath gone before, to greet us on the blissful shore.*

It was the family's first tragedy. There would be more.

Paha's development began when Judge Clark Long, renowned locally as an Indian fighter and frontier jurist, evolved into a land speculator and bought the townsite from the railroad. He opened his own general store, and put out railroad and newspaper ads for the place. That was in 1889, the year also that Gustav and Pauline Plager, emigrants from Germany, homesteaded a mile northeast up the coulee from the intended new town. Like the Savage family, the Plagers had stopped first in Illinois, where they farmed, and Gustav worked also as a shoemaker. They, too, were wooed by the lure of the West, and so entrained for the Northern Pacific's promised lands.

Unlike the Savage family, the Plagers' six children were born after settlement at Paha. Differently, too, the Plagers' progress, despite some hard losses, broke through the curve of Paha's decline.

Initially, the town grew handsomely, propelling settlers' fortunes along with it. In relatively short order, Paha's two dirt streets acquired a hardware store, a lumber yard, barber shop, two grain-buying agencies, a pool hall, hotel, meat market, dance hall, two saloons, a bank, a brothel, and a newspaper—the *Paha Hub*, a name boastfully reflecting the town's claim to central importance in the county. Alongside the tracks, grain storage warehouses sprouted—the long, low "flathouse" variety common when wheat was still sacked and stacked rather than handled loose. Turn-of-the-century photographs of Paha's burgeoning commercial strip show a movie set-like row of wood frame, false-fronted one- and two-story clapboard buildings, equipped with awnings to roll out over the wooden sidewalks. One of these stores was Lem Jones's newer, bigger emporium, where he also ran the post office, and was doing right well. The dirt road crossing the rails at the depot had been graded up both slopes of the coulee and on out into the fields, and farmers closer to Paha than to Lind or Ritzville were bringing in their crops.

Then, capping this surge of growth, came an apparent guarantee of success: in 1900, the Cummin brothers added a tall, full-scale flour mill to the trackside flathouses. It employed twenty men, a real industrial anchor for local hopes. Before long, the mill was grinding hundreds of thousands of bushels of wheat into prize-winning "Silver Loaf" and "Gold Standard" flour, shipped literally worldwide. In a flourish of confidence, the town raised a big brick schoolhouse, Paha's first masonry structure. The only amenity missing was a church: as one early resident put it, "It was too rowdy, too many drunks to allow a church to come into Paha." Population had swelled to 600 or so in the electoral precinct (which included surrounding farms), competitively close to Lind's 761, and local leaders were eyeing incorporation and a possible claim to the county seat.

The Plager and Savage families both prospered along with the town. It helped greatly that a freak succession of good rain years commenced in 1895, putting local land values on the escalator. Allen Savage and son James particularly set out to profit from this rising market—sometimes in competition with each other. The Savages' real estate ventures were significant. In 1901, for instance, Allen Sr. paid $2,500 in gold coin for a half-section, 320 acres. He and Mary Ann made a profit of $1,400 in the same year on a quarter he'd bought two years prior for $200. In 1905, James sold for $9,600 three quarters that he'd bought earlier for a total of $331. All told, at one time or another, the Savage men held title to 2,700 acres—the equivalent of 4 1/4 sections of land in the township around Paha, a massive amount at a time when the average farm was 300 acres or less.

The edgy relationship between Allen Sr. and James got an official depiction in the 1900 census, when the family was for some reason living in a house in Lind. Allen Sr. was listed as head of family. Although James was recorded as a bachelor, he identified himself also as head of family.

James had become the lead son when his older brother William endured the family's second tragedy. Working for hire on another farm, he was gravely wounded by an unspecified blow to the head. He became a delusional epileptic, and his fellow farm workers feared him as a danger to himself as well as to them. In 1892 he was committed to the newly opened Eastern

State Hospital for the Insane in Medical Lake, fifty miles north of Paha toward Spokane. In sad evidence of how benighted the rural medical world was those days, the examining doctors noted the blow to his head, but in response to the committal form's question "Supposed cause of insanity?" they wrote "Most likely masturbation." (Alienists of that era clearly were convinced that sexual self-gratification had strong impact on the psyche. A previous question on the form asked whether the insane person was "addicted to masturbation." The doctors answered, "unknown.")

Hospital staff recorded that William was often irritable between his convulsions, and no wonder. His principal delusion was that his ribs and back, and sometimes all the bones in his body, were broken.

Pat Brison, granddaughter of the Savages' fourth child, Cora Belle, and a resident of California, sent me copies of her cache of early family photographs. The earliest are from the late 1870s, in Illinois. These studio portraits show that the parents (who also had likenesses taken) cared enough to have their children's images recorded at various ages, and likewise had the disposable cash to pay for it. And the apparel worn after they reached Adams County indicates that they had money not only for such relative luxuries but for the proper—and sometimes stylish—attire that pride would require for such depictions.

A group shot of the four oldest siblings earlier in 1879 or '80 portrays them in neat, serviceable clothing, not special, but not plain. Here are the only images of William and Salena, grouped formally with James and Cora Belle somewhere in Illinois. William, probably eleven, is a budding image of his father. Salena, four years younger, wears a jumper over a long-sleeved dress. She looks fresh, interested, intelligent in her emerging girlhood. She is not sickly—indeed, seems to be holding energy in check.

Her expression is intent, perhaps faintly amused. Straight, dark hair (goodbye to my image of Debussy's golden-haired maid), center-parted and pulled back to fall behind her ears, is cut just above the collar. Grown up, she would probably have resembled her sisters, comely women with strong, attractive faces featuring —courtesy of their father—remarkably square chins.

Salena is looking straight at the camera, straight at me. I return her gaze for long minutes, imprinting her face in my memory. Too soon, she would die.

In the next photo, her father also gazes straight out: Allen Sr. of the wide-set eyes, mutton chop whiskers, and possibly petulant lower lip. He presents a bit of flash: a stylish ribbon bowtie encircles his tall collar, the snowy shirt front below highlighted by the plunging V of his vest beneath a dark, well-fitted suit coat. The ensemble adds authority to a broad, strong, handsome face that would have been very forceful in anger.

Mary Ann, by contrast, a mother then in her thirties, appears in a voluminous, all-covering plain dark dress with only the faintest hint of decoration at the narrow collar. Her expression is as severe as her tightly drawn back, center-parted dark hair.

But she changes. In her sixties, in Adams County, her silver coiffure is done in soft braids that run back just above her ears. Her expression is still firm, but pleasantly so, with the hint of a smile. What shows of her dark dress looks stylish: double light stripes run up to a mandarin collar, and a ruffle swoops across from shoulder to shoulder. A small, gay, cinched kerchief is attached above her bosom like a corsage.

The remaining children, now ranging from early twenties to early thirties in age, likewise appear in genteel parlor clothes: three-piece suits on the sons, Cora Belle and Martha in puff-shouldered white blouses above dark long skirts, their hair fashionably rolled up.

These were money years, the time of expensive apparel. Allen Sr. had bought three house lots in Ritzville, and he and Mary Ann moved to a residence there. But these years must have been times of tension as well, because there was considerable leveraging under many of the big land purchases. The wheatland that James got so cheaply and later sold so dear, for instance, paid him when he leased it out, but not enough to offset the two mortgages it carried. Allen Sr., eager always to expand his estate, also borrowed from the bank when he added acreage—including two half-sections adjoining the original homestead. The secondary price that both men paid in their financial balancing act was the vulnerability of heavy debt.

The family, like the town, was doing well on borrowed time. In retrospect, it's tempting to read ominous portent into household troubles brought on by the '90s. In 1899, Cora Belle took her own big risk, and before long was paying dearly for it. She married George Vose, a plumber from Spokane. He turned out to be a violent drunk who beat her both at home and in public. When she fled from him with their child, Roy (Pat Brison's father), he threatened to take the boy away. She found refuge at the old homestead with Martha, Levi, and Allen Jr. And in 1906 she took action both brave and unusual at that time in rural society. With Martha as her witness, she got a restraining order and a divorce.

But next year a blow fell that far overcame the hard emotions of that disentanglement. Mary Ann was killed when a locomotive smashed into her buggy at a grade crossing near Ritzville. Did she misjudge the distance? Imprudently rush ahead? Did the horse bolt? The news reports gave neither information nor opinion. She was sixty-seven years old.

The family began to spin apart. Cora Belle, first to go, moved away after her mother died, and by 1908 had remarried and was living in California. By then, typical low rainfall had returned to Adams County, exacerbated by devastating attacks on wheat crops by squirrels and jackrabbits. The bottom dropped out of the land market, eroding the family's paper fortune. James, his holdings taken by the slump, became a well driller in Prosser, over one hundred miles away to the west.

In 1909, Paha's seeming door to fortune slammed shut: the flour mill closed, outdone by newer facilities in Ritzville. That doomed the town, although the full demise would take some time. But the Savage family children discovered sooner that Allen's ostensible wealth was bringing them an almost equivalent disaster. Allen himself died in 1911, victim of gangrene from a wound he suffered while mending fence on the homestead. His principal legacy turned out to be mortgages that would have to be paid or surrendered.

After his father's death, Allen Jr. headed for Chicago. Levi became an itinerant farmhand, finding himself eventually on a ranch in Post Falls, Idaho, where James joined him. The remaining daughter, Martha, could have simply abandoned the situation and moved elsewhere. Instead, she resolved to keep at least something of the family's property intact.

In the end, all she could save was the Elm Street house in Ritzville. That became home for her and, when she married, her husband, John Johnson, as well.

*　*　*

The Plagers, meanwhile, suffered their own grievous losses. Gustav's wife, Pauline, died in 1907, aged fifty-four. *She was the sunshine of our life.* Three years later, fourteen-year-old daughter Mary followed her—like Salena, another young woman taken far too soon.

But the family economy fared better than that of the neighboring Savages. Gustav, like Allen and James Savage, wanted land, and bought it when he could. He eventually owned three thousand acres, two-thirds in wheat and the rest in pasture. Unlike the Savages, though, Gustav diversified his farming. He planted grain, but he also broke and sold horses, herding as many as 150 at a time. He also kept some 25 head of cattle.

And the Plagers set down family roots. As the surviving children married and took on their own lives elsewhere, one son, Rudolph, stayed home to help run the ranch. When he married Louise Schutz in 1918, she came to live with him at the Paha homestead. Gustav died in 1927, and Rudolph and Louise stayed on, raising their own four children. During the years of the Great Depression, severe drought stifled the Big Bend country as badly as it did the more famous midwestern Dust Bowl. As one local account puts it, "the land blew." Blinding dust storms overwhelmed parched crops, and even smart farming was not enough to sustain the family. Rudolph hired out to work on building the new Route 395, and Louise managed the room and board they provided for some of the road building crew.

The homestead was saved, and much of the land. Rudolph and Louise had three daughters, who married and moved away. But son Wesley, born in 1923, echoed his father and stayed home. Reflecting on his youth in Paha, he recalled that although the town was diminished, it still was a support center for the families around.

When I was a young kid, from seven years on, during the summer, my job was to get on my saddle horse and ride to Paha to pick up the mail. And if there was one or two little items that Ma would want, I'd pick that up. The saloons was closed when I was old enough to ride into Paha. I'd guess there was around fifty people in the town then. The only thing there was the depot and Lem Jones' grocery store, which also had the mail.

And Lem would put a punching bag out, and blindfold you, when you was a kid. And if you could knock that punching bag off that hook, you got a candy bar. Boy, you'd take an awful beating from that punching bag. When you'd punch it, you couldn't see it, and it'd swing around and slap you upside the head. I can only recall getting one candy bar, that I could ever knock it off that hook. But I got knocked in the head a lot of times.

In his trips back and forth, and in his years at the Paha school, Wes saw the physical decline—actually, the recycling of the town. In the 1930s, the saloons, the other store, many houses,

were just sitting there vacant. And my folks, their house was small, so they bought a house in Paha and put it on iron-wheeled wagons with horses and hauled it up to our place, and attached it to their house. Then here and there a guy would come along, and either buy a place or just tear it down for the lumber. During World War II especially, a lot of them went like that to build a house in Ritzville or Lind. Nor was it just houses. I had a friend who bought, or I guess he bought what used to be the old grocery store, tore it down and built a house here in Ritzville with the lumber.

Legend has it that the bank, useless as living space, was likewise uprooted, hauled, and dropped in some distant fold of coulee. No one now knows where. Some buildings burned. New consumer protection regulations targeted the health risk of the grain storage flathouses' openness to rodents and birds, and they were taken apart. A single, vertical wooden elevator replaced them, much less massive in its presence.

The school, its enrollment fading, closed in 1937. And the last bastion, the general store and post office—operated by the Timm family after Lem Jones's death—closed in 1943.

The town literally disappeared.

For a while, though, the socially interconnected community of farm families around Paha survived. Even as some of them gave up their windblown land, the Plagers and others persisted in their long-established patterns of neighboring. Wesley married Joan Anderson in 1950. Her grandfather had emigrated from Denmark in 1906, and she lived in Spokane until age fourteen, when her family moved south. New situations did not faze her, and when she came to live at the homestead, she set out also as Wes's partner in the steady annual round of mutual help, reassurance, and recreation that drew together the remaining Paha-area farming families. As more war came overseas in Korea, the job in this home sector was once again to bring in the crops. The farm families celebrated with each other in the effort. There were picnics at the Paha grove, baseball games. The Paha team— Wes played first base and center field—even traveled to challenge Ralston and other towns. And on weekends, recalls Wes, among the neighbor families "We'd just go here, go there, get together, and play pinochle, four handed pinochle."

The Plagers in retirement were still a lively, handsome couple when I sat to talk with them in 2004 at their latter-day home in Ritzville. Wes, tall, plainspoken, with a friendly, craggy face, was still quite fit after decades of farm work. Joan's Danish heritage showed in her fine Scandinavian features and light brown hair. Her responses were eager, precise, and so involved her that she sometimes stirred in her chair as she spoke.

Their memories were occasionally wistful, but on balance more realistic than sentimental. Along with the parties and friendships, they also told of digging for bottles and other artifacts where Paha's commercial buildings had once stood. And they recalled how technology began to pull apart what card games and dances had brought together.

The Plagers and their neighbors got electricity in 1940, courtesy of the Rural Electrification Administration. At home, it was a great help. Wes recalls that "I'd go out to the barn to milk, and all I had to do was hit this little switch, and I had all kinds of light. Where before I had to pack this old lantern around, hang it on a wire, slide it from one cow to the next."

But along with light bulbs and helpful motors came radio, and later the more serious infiltrator—video. And with that, isolation. "When that television come, and all," says Wes, "people wouldn't go no place, they'd just watch TV."

"Wes's grandmother, I remember," says Joan, "she died in '53, when it was just the test pattern on the television? And she'd call it the *duyvil*. She just thought it was hell coming into the house. Just the devil—they've finally done it."

Arguably, she was right.

* * *

The Savage family missed Paha's endgame, but—for Martha and the surviving sons—only by a matter of miles. Cora Belle was the only child who accomplished a departure both voluntary and permanent: she died at age seventy-five in 1951 and was interred in Richmond, California. William lived out his life in the hospital at Medical Lake, and was buried there in 1926. For the other brothers, Martha's house in Ritzville became the family magnet— that, and Allen Sr.'s grave in the town's memorial cemetery—and it did draw the brothers home. Levi, fifty-two, came back to Elm

Street in January of 1931. He was sick with double pneumonia, and died the day after he arrived. He was buried beside his father. In May of that year, James, sixty, followed Levi into the ground. Allen Jr. completed the backtracking in 1954, although he wasn't alive for the last seventy miles: he died in Spokane at seventy-one, took a final train ride south, and two days later joined his father and brothers at rest in the family plot. Martha, dead in 1966 at age eighty-six, also died in Spokane, where her daughter survived her. But she came home like her brothers. She lies in another part of the Ritzville cemetery, buried under her married surname beside husband John Johnson.

A sadly affecting measure of the family's financial decline is that none of the Savage men's graves in Ritzville has a marker of any kind. Brothers and father repose under anonymous grass.

But that's not so poignant as the fact that no one knows for sure where the mother, Mary Ann, was buried. Allen Sr. dealt with the Ritzville mortician who prepared her body after the accident. But he did not have her interred in the municipal cemetery where gravesites awaited him and his sons. The only hint to where she went is that the undertaker's fee for the hearse that bore her was fifteen dollars, versus the usual ten, indicating it may have traveled an unusual distance.

So the best guess is that she was taken to Paha's cemetery, for which interment records no longer exist. And if so, did Allen's choice of destination express his wish not to share earth with her, or hers to be buried away from him? Or was it a decision by one or both that she should lie beside her eldest daughter?

Impossible to know. One can only hope that the two of them are keeping company there, in the hilltop earth above Paha. Allen provided his wife no marker.

But Wes Plager did.

It's certain that in the early days, the first members of these emigrant families to arrive encountered each other, likely even exchanged pleasantries at Lem Jones's store, perhaps did some business, certainly knew about each other. Wes and Joan have no family memories of that to relay. Nonetheless, the Savages have a niche in the Plager family's abiding connection to the place their forebears shared with all who made the town's history.

Talking with Wes and Joan, I mentioned that some of the graves in the town cemetery had only a narrow, rectangular concrete slab embedded in the ground as marker, with a name hand engraved by some stylus in the wet cement. Did that reflect hard times, when people couldn't even afford to erect a monument for the deceased?

"Yes," said Wes. "My dad made those. When he was already retired and moving into town he poured them little slabs and put the names on of the people he could remember, and him and I put that fence around there." He mused. "When I was a kid, I never thought much about it, Paha disappearing. Just the same way as when I went to school, and then they closed it and it didn't bother me a bit, at that time. I never gave it no thought, until I got older, and I got to thinking golly, I wish Paha still had the stores, and was like it was when I was a kid."

His memories were proactive as well as sentimental. Even after he and Joan themselves retired and moved to town, Wes took up his father's legacy. He and son Rudy—an elected county commissioner, now residing at the family homestead—expanded their attentions beyond the Plager family plot. Sometime after my first visit they weed-whacked the whole cemetery. By the time I went there again, the lowered profile of the felled mustard made the place definitely more respectful of its occupants. But there was more. Research aided by local historian (and pioneer descendant) Irma Gfeller identified yet other unmarked burials.

For those, Wes made simple flat metal crosses, engraving the name on the crosspiece himself.

One was for Mary Ann Savage. Set beside Salena's beautiful stone, it notifies the world that this precious daughter was not abandoned. And that the family of her name was indeed part of the matrix of this place as it expanded, rode high, and then faded away.

4

First Harvest

Wes Plager was seventeen when electricity changed farm life in Adams County, forever and for the better. But that was only the latest of the major technological innovations his young life had experienced. His saddle horse was modern enough transportation to the Paha store and post office. But for farther journeys, "We had an old Oakland. It was a big sedan that had wooden spokes for the wheels. When the Folks'd go to town on Saturday, you'd hear just squeak, squawk, squeak, squawk, as they drove along. So before they left, us kids, my sisters and I, we'd have to get out and water the wheels, let 'em soak up a little bit so they wouldn't squawk so much."

Cars with silent, steel-rimmed wheels would follow, of course. But meanwhile, the family took an even steeper step into new machinery: in the mid-1930s, the Plagers progressed from horses to a gasoline-powered tractor to pull their farming equipment.

This was a crawler, running on continuous, flexible belts of cleated steel plates rather than wheels, a machine of the kind later known to the world as a *cat* for the Caterpillar company that over the years most famously produced them.

Replacing up to thirty horses or mules with one snorting tractor was a transition so stunning that it overshadowed the corollary impact of reducing the need for human labor in the harvest of grain. It wasn't just that all the jobs dealing with herds of draft animals disappeared. The new machines also more speedily winnowed successes and failures among local farmers. Tractors made it possible to crop more land more efficiently—if you could afford the machinery, and if you had the land. These were high thresholds for many local families. Particularly in the dry, dusty 1930s, many stumbled, finding no choice but to follow the departing hired hands to some other place.

The aftereffect was a slow-growing equation: fewer farm workers, fewer farm families, less need for the amenities of town.

As the song has it, you don't know what you've got 'till it's gone.

Almost a century of evolving harvest mechanization had preceded the onset of the Plagers' cat-pulled combine harvester. And there was more to come. But those earlier changes had been quantum leaps. By the time serious wheat farming began in Adams County, the earliest methods of harvest by sickle, and then scythe with cradle, were ancient. But Adams's earliest farmers were still dealing with the latest evolution of the McCormick Reaper—the first mechanical harvester. It was a machine that merely cut down the wheat, needing other workers to follow to collect the mowed grain, and transport it to a place where the kernels could be threshed loose from the stems.

Which was done by yet another new machine. No more the eighteenth-century need to walk cows or horses around on the cut wheat to knock loose the grains. Instead, crews of up to twenty men traveled from farm to farm with enormous steam-engined tractors that arrived like slow and noisy elephants, settled, and powered the newfangled threshing machines via long belts that turned those contraptions' drive gears.

With the blink of a historical eye, these dinosaur machines

were gone, taking operators' jobs with them. Combined harvesters entered the market in the 1920s, machines that both cut and threshed the wheat (and through all their evolutionary improvements are still known by their shortened name, "combine"). Even though they wiped out the steam threshers, these were still labor-intensive devices. The earliest combines needed a crew of at least five on board: a driver who could handle the big team of animals, a "combine man" who tended the machine's moving parts with his wrenches and oil can, a "header puncher" who minded and adjusted the workings of the long, outrigger mower as it moved through the crop. And down below on a side platform, wretchedly breathing the dust of it all, two workers who funneled the threshed wheat into sacks, quickly sewed them closed, and pushed them off to the ground for following wagons to collect.

The sacking jobs disappeared when even newer technology made it possible to move and store the threshed wheat in bulk, without sacks. Trucks—no more wagons—collected loose grain direct from the combines' downspouts. Then they hauled it to the tall trackside elevators that stood where the former broad, low, flat houses had formerly stored the sacked crop.

That's the way it was when I worked for Bob Phillips in the 1957 harvest, more or less midway in the evolution of technology and work force from early days to now. Bob was farming yearly about 5,000 acres of wheat, and he was running a transitional array of three combines: two veteran red-painted International Harvester machines, pulled by D-9 caterpillars, plus one of John Deere's early self-propelled models, spiffy in that company's trademark green. The Internationals by then needed only a crew of two—one combine man and a tractor driver. The John Deere, bellwether of the future, reduced the need for operators to one: the driver.

In keeping with his retention of the elderly tractor-pulled combines, Bob was hiring harvest crews the old way, from the migrant labor stream. Back then, this flow of laborers still consisted mainly of the southern and midwestern whites John Steinbeck wrote about, following the summer sun's northward track through crop after crop—corn, cotton, lettuce, strawberries, whatever ripened first. My three friends and I—Gerry, Bill, and Pete—were interlopers, third-year students from Vermont's Middlebury College, out for income and adventure during the summer break. We were working night shift in a Walla Walla cannery, processing the green pea crop, when we spotted Bob's ad in the paper for harvest truck drivers at the Phillips ranch. With the pea packing about to end, we phoned Bob and lied that, sure, we were experienced truckers. When he told us to come on, we went to the nearest truck dealership and asked idiot questions about the multiple forward gears, the two-speed axle, the hoist mechanism and such. I recall climbing up to twist the steering wheel of one of the trucks, and may even have said "vroom, vroom."

The cannery work was easy to leave—as in a sort of unhappy, nonsleeping dream in which the muscles are worn by the need to stack a conveyor's endless delivery of cardboard cases of cans, the mind is numbed by the racket of machinery, all amidst the pervasive, cloying smell of cooked peas. It was emblematic that on our midnight break, as we sat in our car to eat, all we could get on the radio was the repetitive groaning of interference from the static thrown by the big drive motors inside.

So it was with pleasure that we set off in the daytime, in the open air, up the still undivided Rte. 395, with its occasional daredevil central passing lanes. We were traveling in a 1939 LaSalle, which did add a little verisimilitude to the image we hoped to project as competent itinerants. But we were about to learn that image mattered little in wheat country, where we were going to be immersed in a different microcosm very much made of realities.

We called Bob from Lind in the late afternoon, and he came in to lead us to the ranch. The LaSalle was hard put to keep up with his Ranchero pickup along the narrow, twisting, rough-paved road to Cunningham, where he stopped to point out "our elevator," recipient-to-be of his wheat. Its single tower was impressive, even haughty, high, and aloof, not transmitting anything except its authoritative presence. *And we were supposed to understand this?* Bob thought so. "You'll be hauling to here," he said, and slid back into the Ranchero, Stetson still in place.

Zoom. Next, up an S-curve hill, off that onto a gravel road, and through his dust we soon made out a stand of trees. It was the ranch windbreak, silhouetted against the orange sky of sunset. The greenery lined three sides of an extensive, rectangular compound, with the road as the fourth side. A truck-sized gravel driveway ran a wide *U* around big corrugated metal equipment sheds, a bunkhouse, and other smaller structures. Each arm of that *U* ended at a roadside house.

The mention of "ranch" had led us to expectations different from what we found. The family did herd cattle as well as crop wheat, but the cows were on some far distant pasture, never in evidence. Not here the popped-up mansion of Edna Ferber's *Giant*, nor the improbably commodious log-built headquarters of the Cartwrights on TV's *Bonanza*. No, the Phillips home was, indeed, a 1940s-era brick house of what—*was I learning something?*—had come to be known as ranch style. It sat next to the road, separated from the gravel by a swatch of watered grass and a shade tree, beneath which was a white, openwork wrought-iron bench. The front yard was marked off from the driveway by a low child-proof fence. The scatter of tricycles and toys was reassuring evidence that in coming to this distant, isolated place, we had not totally departed from everyday civilization.

But only Gerry and I would stay. Bob casually announced that two of us were to drive truck at his brother Boyd's nearby ranch. Flips of a coin sent Bill and Pete away, Bill nervously driving his first truck, Pete riding with Bob. Their disappearance down the road was unsettling, adding to the wariness with which we, the relicts, reviewed our new habitat. We were to sleep on cots in one bay of a three-door truck garage. There was a third cot in our garage space if needed for Luther, a spare, sour-faced cat skinner (as the tractor drivers were called) who drove out each day from Lind. Toilet and shower were in the bunk-house across the driveway, where the rest of the crew slept.

That dormitory was a fairly rudimentary and smallish square one-storey building with four beds, mustard-colored walls, the bathroom, and a small "lounge" with a couple of chairs. The four men billeted there were a true assortment: Noble, combine operator, elderly, bald, dumpy, and opinionated; Conrad, also a combine man, whose tan thinness concealed his age, and who hardly ever spoke; gregarious Ross, cat skinner, twenty-something, freckled, with red brush-cut hair; and truck driver Larry, the friendliest member of the crew, a stocky Yakama Indian of about my age, with a ready smile, a sunny disposition, and a boxer's wraparound muscles. Off season, he fought in the ring, and worked out in the Yakima gym of heavyweight contender Pete Rademacher.

But those introductions were for the next day.

That first night, with the cooling, tardy darkness finally coming on, and the warning that we'd be getting up "real early," there seemed nothing to do but try to sleep. Our garage bedroom had a light overhead in the rafters, no good for reading, plus the predictable stale, background aroma of tires, oil and gas—albeit fresh air blew in sometimes emphatically with the door of our bay partway up. It was a very pared-down situation: amenities missing, a long way from home, next day scary in prospect. Marooned, in effect. I was tied down on the cheerless cusp of having to live up to real stuff I'd said I could do, but knew nothing about.

To my relief, albeit temporary, the next morning brought a reprieve. It seemed that the grain lacked one more day of readiness for harvest, so Gerry and I were sent with heavy grub hoes to dig up weeds among the irrigated windbreak trees. That gave us our first experience of the uniquely fertile, loess soil of the region, and the need for shelter from the persistent southwesterly winds that had brought the floury dirt here and shaped its mounded topography.

Wheat and its post-harvest stubble do a passable job of holding this rich, friable soil in place, but can't compare in that regard to the original native grasses and sagebrush. And when the stubble is disked into the ground during the annual round of cultivation, the easily lifted silts are distinctly prey to wind erosion. Improved equipment and technique have lessened this problem, and the grass plantings of the Conservation Reserve Program have reduced the amount of vulnerable surface acreage. So the choking dust storms that once plagued the county are largely history. Nonetheless, to live anywhere in this area is to live always with airborne dust. On the more than many windy days, the sky well above the horizon turns to tan haze. Even in calm air, microscopic soil particles filter down slowly, constantly onto everything: car, hair, anything inside that's exposed to outside air.

Notably, the conifers we were hoeing around were not there for holding the land. Nor even for shade, although whatever of that they did provide was a summer benison. Nor were they merely decorative, even though their dark, needled presence definitely gave the eyes welcome respite from the sunbaked territory beyond. No, these arboreal barriers were, and are, just that, a defense against those unending southwesterlies, and also the backdoor northeasterly storms that bring the winter's coldest weather. One might also call them safeguards of sanity for ranch families whose often chancy prospects might become psychologically unbearable under years of unimpeded wind. Every surviving farmstead here—and even many of the abandoned remnant homesteads—announces itself by an outlying ring of evergreens, starkly rising in the otherwise treeless landscape.

So Gerry's and my first day as ostensible truck drivers was spent doing one of the most ancient, unmechanized chores of agriculture. Over at Boyd Phillips's place, meanwhile, Bill and Pete got similarly rudimentary duty, being assigned to walk through a smallish field of wheat grown for seed, pulling out the scattered, tall volunteer grasses of wild rye. They were the first of us to learn that the velvety appearance of wheat seen from a distance is true deception. The straw stems of the grain are stiff and tough. And the plants grow in tightly spaced rows with furrows between that can turn a careless ankle. One wonders whether the walking was as hard in Robert Burns's old Scottish ballad, "Coming through the Rye." (Later, Bill and Pete also became hunter drivers, carrying .22 rifles in their trucks with which to kill invading jackrabbits—some of the fallen prey later to be served for dinner.)

The other house in Bob Phillips's compound—on the opposite side past the bunkhouse and sheds—was an elderly clapboard structure, probably the farm's original dwelling. Bob's foreman, Curtis, lived there with his wife, Marlene, and her mother. The women cooked for the crew. These were forceful, thick-bodied females, plain-faced and pale, hair severely pulled back into buns. Faded gingham aprons over the most ordinary of clothes, the image of each other except that the mother was graying and wore rimless glasses. They spoke little and always appeared to be angry.

Curtis, on the other hand, was a surprisingly engaging guy, except when he was hung over, or irascibly giving orders. We quickly learned that he was always to be called Curtis, never "Curt." He was a wiry, mid-sized man with fading reddish hair, a face scarred by earlier acne, and an inviting grin. I didn't understand until later that he was always abrupt in the morning before he got to his stash of booze—which wasn't until the day's harvest was in motion, all the equipment rolling. At our first breakfast—so early, so copious, so . . . incredible, actually, what with pot roast, boiled potatoes, eggs, bacon, toast, milk, coffee, pie—he'd let us know just where in the pecking order we were.

We took chairs around a long table. "Good morning," I said.

"New guys," he growled, rubbing a hand through the stubble on his chin.

So . . . minimal speech at breakfast, okay. It was, after all, only 5:30 AM or so. Then, after an interval for bathroom activities, into the trucks. The combine and tractor guys got up in the bed of my blue Chevy hoistback, their shirt midriffs visible through my rear window as they gleefully pounded on the cab roof, the drum effect adding to my worry about the wide play of the gearshift lever, and the minimally understood Hi–Lo axle range switch. But I got us going, and we convoyed down the gravel road behind Curtis's pickup, eating his dust as we headed for the day's field.

I remember the sweet innocent pleasure of beginning to feel that I could actually do this job. The truck, fairly new and responsive, seemed possible to get acquainted with. Its weight and the authoritative, shushing dual-drive wheels plowed us straight through the road's deep gravel. When we parked at the staging area where the combines sat, and our rolling dust cloud settled, the air was cool, fresh and clean, tinged intriguingly by the brown undersmell of dusty soil and sharper hints of oil and grease from the machines.

We were surrounded by a vastness, and a great stillness. Our equipment was gathered in a kind of dry swale, at a crossroads, on a mowed corner of a field that Noble said was almost a full section, most of a square mile. Square, perhaps, but not level. From our stationary vantage point the land rolled up gently all around in immense, supple mounds and rounded ridges, covered in the corduroy bristle, the delicious light toast color and texture of ripe wheat. There were no trees anywhere, and the only sign of life, other than the roads, was the pole-to-pole droop of a telephone line, disappearing toward our home compound, only a few miles away but as quickly invisible as though swallowed. The sky, correctly and unexceptionally blue, stretched around so routinely that the eye dismissed it in favor of the more interesting land forms.

There was the slight crink of cooling truck engines. Larry and John leaned on a fender, smoking, desultorily talking. The urge to converse seemed a violation of the quiet, and when words came out they were hushed. Gerry and I had our first close-up of the combines, enormous, hump-backed red International Harvester contraptions set on broad, tall, spoked steel wheels. The back ends had mysterious horizontal propellors under hoods. *Lift? Lift-off?* Their rising sheet metal sides sported a mechanic's nightmare array of pulleys, belts, levers, and conduit. Noble had climbed up on one of the combines to poke around in his roost, a kind of flat-roofed open shed next to the onboard engine, with the grain bin behind. A dumping spout hung out to one side, and from the other projected an awkwardly long lawnmower reel, poised over a cutter bar and a conveyor belt that brought the clipped-off grain to the machine's internal thresher. Overall, these beefed-up reapers looked like one-wing Rube Goldberg terrestrial airplanes, clumsy but surely competent at what they did. And to be able to do that, each was hitched ahead to its propelling caterpillar tractor.

Amazing. And at any other time, fascinating. But I was anxious to know what came next: Curtis had wandered over to the edge of the uncut wheat, twenty yards away, where he stood, smoking, his back to us. Meditation? Rejection? I consulted Larry.

"What're we waiting for?"

"He's gotta tell when the dew's gone off the wheat," said Larry. "Can't cut 'till then." And after I wondered a little longer about that, Curtis started back toward us, barking "OK, let's go."

Combine and tractor engines groaned and coughed into life. Four blue columns of diesel exhaust rose straight up in the air, and finally we rookies got our instructions:

"We dump combines on the move here," said Curtis. "Saves a lot of time. Just ease in alongside and get the pace, getcher bed up under the spout. Keep a look out that back window so's you see it's getting in ok. When he's done, peel off and wait." He dropped his smoke, and stamped the butt into the ground. "Three dumps and you're full, take it on in to the elevator. They'll tell you what to do. And then get your ass back up here for more. Understand?"

"Sure," I lied. Aside from the gibberish I'd just heard, neither of the adjoining roads was the one we'd taken to the ranch from Cunningham, where we'd been shown the elevator. Could I find it? And did I really remember the dumping procedures, other than never to get any part of my body under the truck bed when the hoist had it lifted? Some guy over at another ranch got his arm pinched off when the goddamn thing broke and fell, yeah, and another guy somewhere else got his skull popped. . . . *Great. Tell me more.*

Larry and John left for another field, where John would drive the self-propelled John Deere pusher, with Larry to truck the grain away. Gerry was told to stick around while Conrad's onboard engine got some last minute maintenance. It had coughed into silence. So when Ross pulled Noble's waddling rig out to begin cutting, Curtis said, "Come on, Turner."

I was to be stationed elsewhere—pretty far elsewhere, as it turned out, uphill on the crossroad and well out of sight of the assembly area, with a hip-shaped rise between us. Finally Curtis stopped, his dust cloud and then mine engulfing him as he walked back to talk to me, cursing and fanning with his hand. "Park in there," he said, pointing across a dirt fill in the roadside ditch. "He'll be along in 'bout half an hour. Dump him here and then get Conrad when he comes. Your buddy there's gonna get them on the other side, and you catch 'em here. If you don't get back from the elevator in time, they'll be waiting. So get your ass back up here, you hear?"

"Yeah, yeah," I said.

Then he was gone. I gingerly drove the truck across the narrow fill into the cleared strip the pusher combine had cut around the outside edges to open the field. For the first time I encountered the jounce factor of the corrugated rows of sheared wheat, the steering's uneasiness as the wheels pushed across slick stubble and sank into the powdery soil. Parked then where Curtis had said I should wait, with the engine switched off, the silence spread immediately to fill the big space around my aloneness, everything a bit more ominous now than awesome. The rush of confidence I'd so recently felt faded into apprehension, fueled particularly by Larry's smiling, mystifying advice about dumping the combine. "It'll nerve you up, first time," he'd said. "But there's nothin' to it. Get in low range and aim at the side wheel there, and nose in slow while you're rounding it. Close your window! You'll think you're too close, but you won't be, it just feels funny. And remember, that combine ain't going nowhere but forward. It ain't gonna hit you unless *you* hit *it*!" His friendly fist to my biceps would have felt better had it been inside a boxing glove.

Aim at the wheel? *Close your window?* Why, since the day clearly was going to be hot? Too soon, really, I heard the faint clanking of the approaching machinery.

* * *

Ross made a rubbery face at me as his plodding yellow tractor pulled the somehow larger, suddenly baleful red bulk of the combine into and onward through my windshield's view. The machine had been big enough, hulking, just to stand beside. Now, the giant metal wheels were rolling, and every visible part on my side of it was moving, jittering, turning. An obviously impatient Noble leaned out over his safety rail, gesturing me to come on. Engine and pulley and other mechanized sounds were too loud by far for me to hear him, but the meaning was clear. And I was mesmerized. Drive right next to this wallowing monster, in a truck I hardly knew the width of? And *damn! Damn!* I was cranking the window up as fast as I could to block the sudden blizzard of chaff and dust blown out by the no longer mysterious rear-end propellor. Flying straw was ticking hard against the hood and windows with the sound of a fast, forceful typewriter. A thick mixture of wheat plant parts and the tan soil dust of the field was plastering on the windshield like dark heavy snow, the amount blowing away slightly less always than the accumulation slowly shrinking my forward vision. Windshield wipers seemed wrong, and hardly helped. Sweating now in the sealed-up cab. Hands clenched on the steering wheel. Crazy to drive into this mess, but no choice. *First gear, low range on the axle*, thank you Larry—the truck would creep along without bucking, merciful because I couldn't hear the engine. *Aim at the wheel.* Thanks again, except I could hardly see it, and as the nose of the truck probed in through the surge and whirl, the combine's rolling metal tire grew forebodingly larger in the blowing murk. Big and unforgiving enough, clearly, to do major damage to the truck should I screw up, particularly hurtful to the thin metal door skin that ostensibly shielded me. But I was edging ahead of the wheel now, out of the blizzard, tension easing slightly but still strong because, as Larry had warned, it did feel funny—worse than funny, *scary*—driving close in to this machine that loomed like a moving house beside me, my truck lurching as it navigated the hump and trough of the wheat rows. And Curtis's directive to monitor the ongoing dump through the rear window obviously required driving one-handed, one arm atop the seat back so I could look behind at the grain spouting down instead of forward toward my doom. It felt insane to take my eyes off the frontal progress.

But I did, and the cascading wheat was indeed spreading its slippery pile in just about the middle of the bed. The downflow began to taper off. Ceased. And I steered away to a trembling stop, watching as the combine's exhaust propellor's dust storm caught up with me again, then moved on, its dispersal lowering and lessening in perspective until I could again see the rear and the jiggering belt-pulley side of the harvester. And then, as the elephantine parade of cat and combine plodded ahead, pulling away its noise and turbulent miasma, the big header reel came in view out on the combine's other side. Compared to the crazed mechanization of the dumping side of the machine, this turning set of vanes seemed staid, placid, so calmly bending the wheat into the cutter bar to be snipped, and conveyed, and threshed, as the rig reaped inexorably on through the field. With distance, as the harsh sound and blasting dust cloud moved away, the reaping took on a sedateness much more appropriate to the dignity of this ancient process than the fright ride I had just experienced. The calming beat of my heart found a satisfaction in the slow but departing forward speed of the machinery. It was my first experience of the self-justifying, almost hypnotizing tendency to want to watch these machines performing, even from afar.

* * *

The heat had increased as the morning progressed, the truck's closed-up cab particularly stifling during the unloading. It was a relief to be outside. So it was with pleasure that I'd climbed up into the bed following the dump, as Curtis had instructed, to level off the load with the big scoop shovel that rode along with a broom on the truck bed's sideboards. The wheat was like solid water, giving ready access as I thrust the shovel in, then slipping fast and silky off the blade to spill its cascading batter-tan grains elsewhere, hissing in renewed contact with the load, emitting the faint scent of edibility as it flowed.

And then came time to go to the elevator. The loaded truck was different, reluctant to move, emitting groans and flexing sounds as it labored through the soft soil to the road. I had become important: protector and deliverer of these tons of most basic stuff. Now I would complete the next step toward bread, taking the wheat to its handlers. The truck was asking me to work with it, use the gears and axle ranges best, and I was learning. And the brakes—thanks be that they were good, because the final run to the elevator was down that long, S-curved hill into the Providence Coulee. That's where I learned that governing a multi-ton load was really quite different than slowing down a car. So on the first trip I didn't have the spare attention to enjoy the textures of the passing grassland, the purling of air through the side windows, now mercifully open, the mixed smell of hot metal and dirt dust, the sounds and force of the engine when I'd learned my gears right. That came later.

The downhill returned me to the tiny town of Cunningham, on the railroad. The Phillips family had built its own elevator there, the one Bob had pointed out on our arrival trip out to the ranch. It was a gaunt, square-sided wooden tower, weathered deep brown, that loomed up to a peaked shed atop. A slant-roofed addition projected out from one wall, receiving a driveway through a gaping truck-sized door. The whole of it contrasted considerably with the town's remaining scatter of low-rise houses and the residual store, whose cold, liquid reward would soon be revealed.

I was grateful for the number of loads ahead of me, giving me the chance to watch and learn. It was a friendly scene—drivers out of their trucks as they waited, talking or shouting to each other until the line moved. When I got close to the shed, a guy a little younger and smaller, but muscular, came up smiling as I waited outside my cab.

"Want to wrestle?" he said.

Quick consideration: was this some sort of necessary local test? I hadn't seen anyone else wrestling, and it was about the last thing I wanted to do. But . . . say no, and be shamed?

The truck ahead moved. "Maybe next time," I said, climbing back in.

And then came the real test: maneuver through the square door into darkness, not scraping either side, onto the weighing platform in the sudden gloom. A squat man with glasses, sitting behind a lighted window to my left, marked down the truck's loaded weight, then gestured me to get out and dump. So, back to the rear, open the square slide-up gate, see the first flows of grain run down into the receiving pit through the slotted center opening in the weighing platform. Then—*oh, do it right!*—climb back in to activate the hoist, the whole bed groaning upward in a sharp tilt, spilling the load in a fine, thick stream out the back.

Of course, I raised it too high, the window man rolling his eyes as my truck bed's upper corner crunched a rafter of the overhead slanty roof. But the wood there had already been gouged: I was not the first. So I shrugged, hopped down to sweep out the residue collected against the now nearly horizontal tailgate, then lowered the damn thing down. Big clank. Got back in to be weighed empty, then waited for the gesture to leave. And just like coming from a tunnel, there I was again, out in the bright. And lo, the wrestling kid was waiting, holding up an air hose.

"You'll want to blow it out," he said.

What?

"Crack the hood," he said. "I'll do it for you."

So I pulled the hood lever, got out, and learned how to blast away chaff trapped in the radiator, so the truck wouldn't overheat. And I learned, too, that I really hadn't been mistaken—I *had* hit some of the little birds that launch up from the weeds beside these farm roads. I'd come to think of them as moron birds because, when disturbed, many fly directly in front of the intruding vehicle, rather than away from it. Little taupe and grey birds, name unknown to those who kill them. "What are they? Field birds, I guess," said one farmer. (I've since learned that they are a species of sparrow.)

On that first run, there were two of them, immolated on my radiator: plastered there in feathery wreckage until blown away by the artificial wind of compressed air, skittering off to join the detritus of chaff and straw that the real winds would spread around into invisibility. Goodbye, birds.

And on that first trip back to the field, I drove, uninformed, away from the little store that Ross later told us sold beer. Subsequently, on some runs I would stop there. The perpetually unsmiling elderly couple who ran the place, tidy in their white aprons and tight-eyed glasses, were less than impressed by my appearance and mission. They stood silently, disapprovingly behind the glass-fronted, butcher-style display case that featured little more than cold 3.2% Olympia beer—the strongest the state then would permit. In the worst of the afternoon heat, I would get three, sometimes four, from their reproachful (but willing) hands. Crack one open on the way back up the hill to slake the dust away, the others for Gerry and Ross when I found them again in the field. Gerry would do the same on his runs. Cold, delicious, even though weak and wimpy in modern terms: situationally, the best beer I've ever had.

But I obtained no beer that first day, and none was needed for the euphoria that began after I got back to the field. Parked on the ridge, with no combine in sight or earshot, I climbed up to sit on the top of my cab. Looking down and out upon this place, this vast sward of wheatland, where I had just established my right to be, I was captivated.

The sensuousness was powerful. The dry air pleasantly parched away my sweat. Light breezes, ruffling past my ears, moved down the slope to press fans of bending response into the uncut wheat. The land spread away voluptuously, its rounded upthrusts and soft swales like primal sculpting of the feminine form. Wonderfully edible, too. The interaction of summer heat and young male hormones added subliminal arousal to this sensory influx.

A stillness of longing filled me, a sense of suspension. It occurred to me with what seemed great propriety that I was very much alone. A lament my father used to sing rose to memory, about a "nice young man" who, going to the hay meadow "for to mow," felt a snake bite his heel and

. . . fell on the ground
And as he lay there, looked around
To see if anybody he mout spy
To carry him home where he mout die
He mout die

The raw old Appalachian tune evoked a curious, neutral realization: were I to die on the spot, no one would see or know. In that time-stopped moment, somehow the thought was . . . acceptable. From the vantage point of my youth and the elevation of the rise, it seemed to me that the land and I were in a state of mutual possession. Joining it would be a contentment, a spread into the infinite. The sense was of comfort and absorption, not loneliness or fear.

The distant sound of the approaching combine brought me an upwelling of satisfaction: a feeling of immersion in the great sweep of agriculture, rolling on down from the first planting of grain. Young as I was, I was still open to the possibility of plumbing the forces of history. It was a conceit that was soon submerged under the reality of grueling, hot, dirty harvest work. But the yearning surge of it would never entirely disappear.

*   *   *

There were relaxations in those harvest weeks, though, along with the hard work. Luther went home to Lind every night, and the other older men on the crew kept largely to themselves after dinner—either in their bunk rooms or heading off to town—but Ross, Larry, Gerry and I, the young guys, had become a social foursome. We'd sit around in the garage or in the bunkhouse lounge, shooting the shit or playing cards.

Ross emerged as the leading light amongst us as regards joie de vivre. High school dropout, perhaps—he never said—odd-jobbing his way along. Good-natured, liked to laugh. Liked to be the center of attention—in that context, a tolerable kind of showoff. Liked to do whatever he felt like doing and, mostly, to hell with the consequences.

Sometimes we'd go into Lind to booze a little. And one of those trips on a Saturday night showed us a new facet of Ross's relatively manic personality. We had convoyed, Ross in his beat-up Ford with Larry along and us following in the LaSalle. Drank some beers in a bar crowded with harvest guys, and desperately few females. Tiring of that, we decided to take a case of bottles back to the bunkhouse and just hang around for a while.

Ross led out, and drove fast as he always did. And he decided to play chase. So we hared off after him onto gravel where, before long, we saw his brake lights flare through the dust. His right rear tire had blown. He had no spare, of course. Get in with us, we said, we've got enough room. Leave the car here and we'll figure something out tomorrow.

No way, said Ross. He thought bad things would happen to his Ford overnight (in retrospect, I guess that was because he had been the cause of some such bad happenings himself). "I'll just drive 'er on back," he said.

"I'll get in with you guys," said Larry.

So we proceeded at chastened speed, the dust reduced enough that our headlights showed Ross's flattened tire as it flobbered joltingly around the rim. Chewed up pieces began to fling away. Then with an explosive relief the whole body of it separated, bounding off into a field. There was nothing then but the wheel rim, digging into the gravel as the car listed strongly to the right.

How the rear axle differential on that car handled the situation, I don't know: the naked wheel had to be spinning far faster than its opposite-side twin. But Ross kept on, the rim first becoming shiny from the abrasion, then its flanges diminishing, the polished, lumpen thing hardly recognizable as what it was by the time we reached the ranch.

Ross never even looked at it until the next day.

He was fond of edgy tractor games, too. As his caterpillar ploddingly pulled the combine along into the zone where a truck waited, he'd sometimes step out onto the moving tread, let it carry him a few feet, then jump off. Then trot ahead of the tractor, put his foot up against the front side of a tread cleat just as it went into the ground, let the steel plate press his foot into the soft soil, and stand there, inches from the menacing, moving, dirt-shedding metal belt, hands on hips, making a kid's better-than-you face as the roaring machine continued on over his captured, buried foot. When his chosen plate of the tread reached the rear and began to lift up, he stepped back, walked in pace with the tractor at the rear until ready, then, toeing onto a rising cleat, let the tread carry him up and along to where he could again move off into his seat.

That taught me two things. One, I wasn't going to do any stupid bullshit like that, even though Ross challenged us all to try. And two, so *that*'s how caterpillars work. The treads don't drive the machine—they're just the endless road it lays down to ride on. The tread doesn't propel, merely clutches the ground so that the sprocket wheels can move the machine forward, plate by plate by plate. The breadth and length of the tread spreads the tractor's weight so as to ride and grip the soil, not sink. Tons of tractor cross a single point leaving only a firm impression on the surface—in this case, with Ross's footprint below.

Of course, had there been a serious rock under his foot placement, he'd have been in big trouble. But in these deep, powdery soils, that was extremely unlikely, and he knew it.

* * *

Ross also was infamous at the foreman's house, where we ate. He became the enemy of Marlene and her assisting mother. Theirs was a hard lot during harvest, feeding the crew three times a day. They never sat at table with us, instead stood like a defensive line between the open kitchen and the eating area, arms folded over their expansive breasts, faces set in what seemed to be permanent frowns. Their stance put them just a few feet behind Curtis, he at the head of the long table. They were like monitors at every meal—eat it, or else.

Curtis ignored their presence. But then, his back was toward them. The rest of us had to absorb their glare, shrink away when they added or replaced platters of food. We never saw them outside except when they went shopping. I remember most vividly almost colliding head-on with them in my truck as they went into town to get supplies—Marlene driving fast as hell down the near middle of the gravel, me just barely avoiding the ditch, their expressions through the windshield just as unchangingly grim as at mealtime. Fierce women.

Curtis's inattention undercut some of the negative power they radiated, although god knows much of their sourness might well have come from living with him. But as a mere member of the crew, one's tendency was to placate them, mildly praise the food—which was, after all, copious and satisfactory.

Ross saw it differently. He figured a woman as forbidding as Marlene deserved needling. So he went after her pie, which she provided at every meal. Over the years, I've come to understand that among women who bake, the quality of piecrust is a crucial measure of skill and merit. Ross had learned that before me.

I'd have rated Marlene's piecrust as decent, not great. A little tough, perhaps. But Ross began to feign having trouble cutting through it. At first the teasing was just remarks to others at the table in a loud enough voice ("Geez, this is tough pie! Ain't this crust tough?") No one else would chime in, and Marlene just rolled her eyes. As he kept at it, she began telling him to shut up and eat—a sign of serious displeasure, because Marlene didn't like to talk: doing so revealed her missing front teeth. Then came her attempt to settle things: "Just don't eat it if you don't like it. I don't see nobody else holding back."

So Ross upped the ante. Next day, he brought a hunting knife to breakfast, with which, he announced, he was finally going to conquer the pie. Even Curtis laughed, but Marlene called Ross a shithead and stomped back to the stove, leaving her mother to hold the line. And yes, Ross did use the knife, and complained yet again.

The next day he brought a carpentry saw, and a live-action slapstick sequence broke out. As he sat down, waving the saw, Marlene grabbed her broom. advanced swiftly and began whacking him on the head and shoulders. Ross tried to ward off the blows, but she was determined to give him real punishment. In the end, he had no choice but to scrabble up out of his chair and flee, Marlene smacking his back and rear end as he made for the door and got out. She grabbed the saw from the floor where he'd dropped it, and flung it after him. Slammed the door and, glaring at Curtis, stormed back to the kitchen. Her mother smiled, her face becoming momentarily pleasant—neither of which I had thought possible. At the table we had been dodging the broom swings and laughing. But laughter was suddenly inappropriate now. After craning a hard look at Marlene over his shoulder, Curtis said "OK, no more bullshit about the pie."

Ross obeyed that dictum, but he had a kind of internal pro-

pulsion that constantly drove him toward the limit of any situation, and a cold edge that could be ugly. A week or so after the
breakfast battle, we were at the staging area, waiting for the dew
to burn off. A field mouse, obviously confused beyond measure,
came bumbling along between two rows of stubble, heading
right toward us. Ross scooped it up barehand, smoothly turned
and hurled it powerfully at the door of my truck, from which it
bounced to the ground and lay still. He picked it up again, and
expertly jerking its tail toward its head, split the abdominal skin
and ripped the backbone halfway out. "Oh look," he said, sus-
pending the mouse at eye level from the tail that now rose from
the middle of its back, "she has babies!"

The creature had not died, however, and began writhing,
pawing at its face in agony.

"Ross, damn!" I said.

Gerry shouted "Jesus Christ, Ross, kill the poor bastard!"

Which he did with one more hard throw against the door.
Then tossed the mutilated carcass back into the stubble. "Something will eat that," he said.

* * *

A day or so later, Gerry's truck broke down in the field. Ross
impulsively decided to see if he could push it to the road with his
cat, the combine still in tow. It was a pretty stupid thing to do:
even with the harvester behind, the tractor was powerful enough
to move the half-loaded truck, but it had no attachment on its
front with which to push. So by the time Ross had moved the
truck a little way forward, the cat's radiator grille was severely
dented inward by contact with Gerry's truck bed.

And Ross was fired. In the bunkhouse, we huffed about that,
charging unfairness. He was only trying to help! The cat was not
seriously damaged, still ran fine! Didn't hurt the radiator itself!

But Noble wouldn't have it. "Mind your own business," he said, forcefully enough that we were cowed.

The ever-silent Conrad, however, wasn't buffaloed. He quietly absorbed the protest talk, then abruptly packed his stuff and quit. An aficionado of the old Industrial Workers of the World perhaps? We never knew. So Luther moved over to pull Noble's rig, and Bob hired a hard-praying Christian father-son team to run the second combine and cat. They were strange, kept to themselves, even slept in their car—a Plymouth even older than our LaSalle. And on their second day, the son—seemingly only in his early teens—pulled the combine under a phone wire hanging low enough to knock the dumping spout out of kilter.

There was only a minor bit of cutting left, though, so they were not dismissed.

But that combine was out of commission for a day, so I was sent to get the load of seed wheat and haul it to Beatrice. Although my selection doubtless was by Bob's mental coin toss, I felt good about it—proud to be among the elite of drivers, classed way up from the kid who'd rolled his truck into the field. It was a short-lived enthusiasm.

After another couple of days with the repaired combine back at work, the harvest came to an end. With the cutting and hauling done, we gathered in the bunkhouse where Bob brought us our truckers' pay of $15 per day (the combine and tractor guys got more), and our bonus—a case of beer. He sat and talked with us for a while as we started to consume it. I recounted the story of the upturned truck and the oddly perched driver. "I wonder where they got him," I said.

"Same place I got you," said Bob.

Years later, when my background was being checked for a military security clearance, Bob told the interviewer that I had been "a trouble maker." I received the clearance anyway. We laughed about that when I visited him in the '90s.

Bob's gone now, but my time working for him is still fresh in my mind. We die, but the essence of who we were survives in the memories of the living. On that score, my recollections are of far less importance than those of Bob's children, and friends such as Joan and Wesley Plager. Together with Bob and his wife Lois, they dug for artifacts in the coulees and at the townsite of vanished Paha—helping to unearth and preserve evidence of the earlier days of an ongoing history that they themselves helped to create.

5

Tenacity

L ike the Plagers, the first of the Phillipses to arrive in Adams
County settled early, managed to survive the hard times
that followed, and prospered. In fact, their oldest son—Robert
Hugh, known by both his middle name and his initials, R. H.—
came to own a remarkable amount of land for crops and cattle.

Virgil and Rachel Phillips emigrated from Missouri in 1901,
homesteading on land near the outpost called Providence,
southwest of Lind. They were among the newcomers wooed in
part by record rainfall and harvests in 1897 and following years,
benisons trumpeted by the Northern Pacific Railroad.

For a while, the Phillipses found themselves midway between
two growing towns. Lind had a head start, but Cunningham was
coming on strong—like Paha, initially a place of promise. It was
founded in 1901 by W. R. Cunningham, a preacher and land
promoter, and by 1913 had grown into a blooming local wheat
shipping center, with a population of 500 and a solid phalanx of
stores and shops. Then hard times hit, as the *Ritzville-Adams
County Journal*'s Centennial Edition records:

> At just about the time Cunningham reached its peak of pros-
> perity, the land began to blow and the drought of the next

few years broke not only many of the early settlers, but also the bank and many of the town's businessmen.[1]

Piling worse upon bad, a big fire in 1916 wiped out the commercial center, and the *Journal*'s tale of woe continues:

"Drought-stricken" was the word for Cunningham during the [First World] war years. Many of the residents were so poor they could not even afford candles for their Christmas trees. . . . Cunningham never regained its former prosperity, though the wheatlands around the town brought riches to those few who had hung on through the bad years.[2]

Population had sunk to 89 by 1920. When I rolled in with my loads of Bob Phillips's wheat in 1957, there were probably almost as many people in and around the line of trucks snaked back from the elevator as there were in the town itself. But that elevator was a proof that Hugh Phillips definitely was one of those few who had hung on and done well.

This pioneer son had mettle along with an affinity for land. After riding out the tough postwar years, he began expanding in 1926—and kept on. His son Boyd told my co-adventurist Pete that "During the [Great] Depression, we ate wheat three times a day and my father bought land for 35¢ an acre." (That was the low end: son Bill's daughter Sharon, in *The History of Adams County*, pegs her grandparents' Depression acquisitions at "as little as $5.00 an acre.")

In the same *History*, Hugh's oldest child, daughter Mildred, recounts:

I was born 4-23-20. The next year, we moved to a new ready-cut farmhouse on the home place. Farm life was difficult, conveniences and plumbing minimum, with no electricity. Farm energy was horse, mule, and manpower. Roads were poor and there were no school buses. So my father moved the family to town.[3]

To Lind, that was, amenities in Cunningham by then having gone down the drain. And Lind became a focus of this thriving family—for investment, among other things. The extensive brick, two-storey Phillips block was built there in 1947, with a movie theater and store at street level, apartments and a dance hall above. Aside from the big trackside elevators, it was the preeminent building in town.

Lind had two railroad stations then—the Northern Pacific downtown, near the elevators, and midway up the south bank of the coulee, the Milwaukee Road. Things were so civilized that a bus ran to the Milwaukee depot, with a stop midway at the Rooster's Rest bordello. A brick-walled canyon of commercial buildings—hotels, restaurants, stores—lined the dogleg of Rte. 395 through town.

All of which was a long way from the startup. No one really knows wherefrom came the name Lind. It used to be said that the word meant "water well" in some Scandinavian language. Or that the songstress Jennie Lind, passing through, had given her name out of delight with the place. Neither is true. Somehow, what had been known only as NPRR Well Number 7 got its new identity, and that's that. Accurate municipal knowledge begins with the Neilson brothers, James and Dugal, who opened the first general store there in 1890. What drew these self-absorbed men to such an undefined place is not known, but they clearly saw it as a way to put themselves on the map: they platted the town with north-south streets labeled N-E-I-L-S-O-N. (Cross streets had numbers). Fortunately, development ceased at *S*, preventing the absurdity of two primary ways identified as *N*.

But within that restricted alphabet, Lind had become a magnet. Photographs early in the 1900s show a powerful stretch of big commercial structures along the tracks—lumberyards and other warehousing besides the grain storage flathouses that preceded the elevators. Droves of itinerant workers gathered in the town park, particularly at harvest time, where the growers would stop by to hire. The hotels were built largely to accommodate this flux of labor force as well as commercial travelers, and their accommodations were not four star. "The rooms were advertised in the window, painted on," recalls Myra Horton, a Lind native who began waitressing and bartending there in 1958 (and later became town clerk), "rooms a dollar to three-and-a-half, and we used to laugh that, well, for three-and-a-half you got the sheets."

Myra was tough, evicting drunks as well as serving drinkers. But in that respect, her job was not oppressive. This was—and is—basically a friendly place. In the 1957 harvest year, my last visit there along with the Phillips crew was for the evening of the Harvest Festival. The town was full of life that night, cornshock decorations on the sidewalks, dancing in the street, bars and restaurants full and jovial, movie marquee lit up. People lazed and flowed in all directions. Light shone from hotel windows. You see a town in full flower that way, you think it's town eternal. We didn't know it was actually Lind at its zenith, that the undertow of decline had already begun—and would accelerate with a bang.

A sort of Murphy's law—the worst that can happen, will happen—imposed itself on Lind just as it had on Paha and Cunningham. But fate encountered an unusual resilience in Lind, despite some peculiarly cinematic twists to the onslaught. There was the matter of really bad masonry. Myra described the demise of Carlock's hostelry, across the street from the Phillips block. "There was the hotel, and in the bottom of the hotel they had a variety store at one point in time, and they had a market. But bricks had started to fall off the facade. And they figured, well, this building is going to fall down, and they got in there, and it took a block and tackle to get that thing down, it was [aside from the dangerous front work] so well built." But down it came. And then, catastrophe: "The whole [rest of the] block caught fire one night, and everything burned." The Gateway restaurant and some stores, up in smoke. Nothing left on that side of downtown's main commercial stretch.

The gods of transportation did not help: in fact, they wished a kind of Greek tragedy on the town. The Milwaukee Road, outdone by the Northern Pacific, gave in to competition and investor discontent, literally pulling up its rails and tearing down its stations. Then, as automotive traffic grew, the Northern Pacific stopped passenger service in 1969 (but under the corporately evolved name of Burlington Northern Santa Fe, the railroad still hauls wheat). The four-lane Rte. 395 bypass had double impact. It cut down traffic through the remaining commercial zone to a comparative trickle, adding pain to the shrinkage of retail trade caused by the departure of unneeded farm laborers and some of the families who had employed them. And it created the outward suction of easy high-speed travel to shopping centers even farther away than Ritzville.

Piling misery on top of misery, Mt. St. Helen's erupted in 1981, pouring inches of smothering ash onto Adams County, inundating with particular damage the towns, such as Lind, that had limited economic resources for clearing away this abrasive "snowfall."

And yet, Lind did not die. An insouciant spirit bubbled up that simply would not let the town go under. It helped that although several storefronts closed, some important anchors survived. The longtime signature Golden Grain cafe stayed open, and Slim's added food service to its bar. Jim's market kept on trading. Crucially, the bank reopened in a double-wide trailer (which, as it turned out, was the extent of downtown reconstruction.) Consolidated Grange kept on selling fertilizer. The Co-op store continued to offer farm supplies. And at Loomis Truck & Tractor, the Case/International ag equipment dealership just east of town, big red harvesting machines still populated the capacious roadside sales lot.

Even more important, though, were the efforts of local activists in the Lions Club and others such as councilwoman Carol Kelly, an attractively energetic former high-school teacher who led in creating a nontraditional approach to promoting Lind. Here, amidst the wheat, the tone is wry. The town's website announces that "Lind is not without charm and history." Indeed. Downtown, a dolled-up mannequin alluringly flashes her blond wig and red dress from the window of an empty apartment above Slim's Cafe. She memorializes the Madam of the old Roosters' Nest bordello. The welcome sign out east of town on Rte. 395 has fun with volcanic disaster. "Drop In," it says. "Mt. St. Helens Did!"

But the best evidence of Lind's nonchalance is parked at the outlying rodeo grounds: battered hulks of large, strangely decorated grain harvesters displaying grievous damage that was gleefully inflicted in the name of community spirit. Every year, spurred by the civically-minded Lions, citizens of Lind abandon their typically sedate, mostly Republican ways, and invite serious abuse of this fundamental grain farming equipment in the Combine Demolition Derby, a raucous sendup of the very agronomy that created the town. Retired combines are stripped of their front-end mowing reel and stem-cutting sickle bar. They get a bit of protective armor, plus outlandish paint jobs and ornamentation—huge eyes, teeth, monster and cow heads, Mickey Mouse ears, and the like. They're given fighting names: *Red Baron, Jaws, Big Willie, Mean Gang Green*. They become supersized battlebots. And with their improbably wide (try 18 feet) header mouths bobbling out front in steel grimaces, they're piloted into the arena, roaring and bouncing, to smash each other up in bizarre, elephantine combat.

The Derby is a burst of frolic, a raspberry to the harvest gods, a celebration of survival. It brings in thousands of visitors each June, makes money for improvement projects, and garners national—even international—publicity.

Carol Kelly says the Derby evinces both municipal resourcefulness and cultural aplomb. "Lind has a sense of humor, all right. We have to. You have to laugh off what you don't have. And there's nothing to do here except what we do for ourselves. But we've got a lot of stubborn pride. There's a bunch of people who work their guts out to make the Derby an event the town can be proud of. This is how we make Lind known to the nation." That's not all, though. Kelly, who handles the Derby publicity (and crewed for the women's combine when it competed, but more on that later), also notes the extra added ingredient that lifts the Derby above the level of just a real-life video game: "It's farmers making entertainment out of their lifeblood." In other words, an enactment of the time-honored, worldwide tradition of agricultural passion plays—in burlesque.

In this context, Lindites should be grateful that their local crop is wheat, rather than the tomatoes that, with equivalent glee, denizens of Buñol, Spain, annually hurl at each other and mash into slop throughout the town. Or the million-plus oranges flung during the yearly carnival by symbolically warring teams in Ivrea, Italy. Crashing combines is cleaner fun by far; yet, like Europe's fruit and salsa fests, it's a spectacle that also gives vent to frustrations of farming—in this case, the tensions of the human/machine interface.

As one Derby crew member explained to a newspaper reporter: "I don't think anyone unless they've driven a combine can understand the thrill of trashing one."

Historically, the Derby was an afterthought. For decades, there'd been a town-sponsored annual rodeo, followed by a parade and picnic—remember that this was stock-raising country first, and cowboys roping and riding bucking critters is showy and thrilling. Celebration of the more mundane grain farming—strongly predominant in local agriculture since early in the twentieth century—took the form of harvest dinners and dances, plus tractor and horse-team weight pulling competitions, equipment displays, and crop-related exhibits at the Wheatlands Fair in Ritzville. As the centennial approached in 1986, however, concern about the town's condition spurred a breakthrough. There was to be a major to-do on that occasion, of course—dedication of a monument, a time capsule, a sculpture, a plaque. A special parade. But somehow all that wasn't enough to commemorate one hundred years' persistence of this town through good times and bad, and to show its vitality. So, people just naturally fired up their old combines and started colliding.

Well, no. It was the Lions Club that added the mechanical rampage to the festive mix. More than any other entity, this organization of farmers and businessmen, motto "We Serve," provides the civic glue that holds together Lind's dispersed community and gives it purpose. By tradition, its membership is male with auxiliary support from spouses. Even with that subtraction of competence, it's a truly versatile group. Farmers, particularly, are skilled in trades ranging from welding and construction to excavation and engine mechanics—and cooking. Both men and women produce and serve the food sold at the Derby to increase the dollar take. In practice, responsibility is copiously shared by both genders when it comes to projects. And there are many of these, all to pump up the town while raising money for groups whose activities sustain the social fabric. Lions give backing to the Scouting groups, Little League, and the Junior Miss competition. They provide and install the town's decorative poles for seasonal flags and decorations. The club helped pay for the roof on the as yet unfunded historical museum, and bought and upgraded the parade Float Committee's trailer. For long years, they've organized the rodeo. Then, the Demolition Derby, which quickly began to outdraw the rodeo. So they constructed all-weather metal bleachers. Those reached their limit of accommodation in 2004, when four thousand people—tourists from Canada, California, the Midwest, many places, as well as locals—came to the show. So the club built yet one more bank of seats.

When the Lions cooked up the Derby idea, therefore, the mayhem was predictably well organized, and well staged. There are safety rules, speed limits, an age threshold of eighteen for drivers. Referees are set to call fouls and disqualify bad actors.

And then the fun begins. The comically decorated combines, all aged fifteen years or older, waddle into the rodeo arena for three very loud, frantic fifteen-minute heats of combat. Five to six combines at a time, engines blaring, bash each other head to head, head to side, to rear, rending metal, popping tires, mixing clouds of dust with diesel exhaust. In between heats, pit crews desperately pound and weld, repairing (if they can) the damaged machines for further action. The last combine moving is the winner. There are cash awards for best decorated, for winning a heat, for the final triumph. But these are inconsequential in both size and importance. As everyone involved will tell you, the event is for the community—as a source of revenue for the beloved Lions, and as a calling card to the world.

In keeping with Lind quirks, the leading Lion who conceived the Derby is affectionately known as Captain Hook. That's Bill Loomis, the septuagenarian proprietor of Loomis Truck & Tractor. He's a craggy, deep-voiced individual with a ready smile— and a prosthetic hook ending his right arm. Loomis, who also farms a considerable acreage of wheat, is an avid outdoorsman. On a hunting trip, recalls a friend, "Someone thought he was an elk, and shot him. Twice." Loomis lost his right eye as well as part of his arm. But he gained a rather sublime philosophy: "As I was lying there on the mountain, I decided that if I got out of it alive, I wasn't going to let the injuries bother me, and I never have." Which means, among other things, that hook, glass eye and all, he drove in the Derby for nine years before an unrelated accident broke his back again (the first break was many years before, when he crashed his helicopter).

"Oh, I loved the Derby driving," he says. "You get wrapped up in it. I hated to quit. People said I was grinning all the time I was out there. It's great sport."

And more. Tanned, animated Frank Bren, who works at Union Elevator and drives in the Derby, says, "Beforehand, my guts just get tied up, I'm so nervous. But when you start driving, the adrenaline rush, well, I tell people it's almost better than sex. *Almost!*"

Bren's combine, painted red and yellow, is named *USMC* in honor of his son in the Marine Corps. Farmer Grant Miller, who won top honors in 2001 in the shark-finned *Jaws*, describes the experience as "better than the best amusement park ride."

Scary? Nah. "Like a carnival ride," says Miller, a squarely solid man with an infectious grin. "Once it gets going . . . or like in football, you've got to get that first hit, then it's ok."

"A lot like bumper cars," echoes Chris Olson, the easygoing creator and driver of pink, floppy-eared, curly-tailed *Porker Express*—"but way better."

Olson's work in "big demolition, tearing things down" makes him a natural for Derby driving. But for others in this farming territory, the context is curious: the Derby, after all, reverses the agricultural tradition of competitions that demonstrate excellence in husbandry and practice. It's the antithesis, for instance, of the much denigrated tractor pull (and its predecessors featuring teams of draft horses, mules, or oxen); the reverse of rodeo demonstrations of skill in work tasks such as catching and subduing cattle, breaking horses, etc. In fact, the Derby, if translated into rodeo, would require cowboys to try to unseat each other by jousting, or cutting an opponent's saddle cinch.

So . . . *why?*

"Well," said Bill Loomis, "pretty near everyone in life has something they'd like to run over a bluff—your car, whatever. With this machinery, farmers are always having problems."

Even farmers' sons can testify to that—Josh Knodel, for instance. High-school buddies Josh and Matt Miller did the restoring, repairing, and brace welding needed to turn a decades-old John Deere model 6602 into the 2001 winner *Jaws* that Matt's father, Grant, drove. Josh eagerly anticipated getting behind the resuscitated combine's wheel to compete for the first time in the 2003 Derby. "I've been driving and fixing combines for years," he said, with a fierce grin. "Now I get to *destroy* one!" *Jaws* came out in bright blue paint that year, dorsal fin high as ever, with the limp legs of a dummy protruding from the grain intake in the header (itself decorated with jagged teeth). He competed well, but got his drive wheels hung off the ground in a collision with a competitor whose machine expired in the process. Unable to move despite still having full power, he lost his heat. But in 2004, Matt, by then eighteen, won shared top honors in the once again rejuvenated great blue mechanical shark.

And recall the crew member's adage that only those who've operated combines can truly understand the pleasure of destroying them. To get the feel of this conflicted man/machine relationship, imagine putting a glassed-in little closet atop your living room, then driving the damn thing 105 times around a half-mile high-school track, wheeling precisely along the edge at five miles per hour. Boring? Throw in the hypnotic turning of the header reel out front, the endless onset of standing grain, the vibration as you drive across the rows, the steady thrum of the engine. Still boring? Yup. That equals the number of passes a typical modern combine makes to cut a quarter-section field (160 acres), medium size around Lind. Fifty-two and a half miles, at least ten hours, if there's only one combine. Now do it again until you've harvested, say, 3,000 acres, or even only that share of the work performed by one combine among several. And again next year, and on. But bless the evolution of closed cabs, pneumatic seats, air conditioning and stereo—as late as my harvest work in 1957, the guys driving the tractor and up on the combine were steadily immersed in the heat, the dust, and the racketing noise of their day-long passage.

Clearly, cartooning and abusing these machines is symbolic of a classic love-hate relationship that's played out in every harvest. But that sort of analysis takes a back seat in Lind. "Really," says Bill Loomis, "It's just fun."

Of course, what's fun in Lind can be a bit offbeat for the rest of the country, particularly since it involves the element of physical risk, plus certain misery. "It's amazing how many aches and pains you have the next day," says Jerry Schuler, a tire shop worker whose truly large size in all dimensions makes him look as invulnerable as his 2003 combine's namesake, *Godzilla*. Thus far, though, no participants have been hurt beyond such day-after soreness. Mike Doyle, the lanky service manager at Loomis Truck & Tractor who frequently has coordinated the Derby for the Lions, emphasizes the safety rules: Protective cages required around drivers' high, exposed perches. Batteries encased, fuel tanks protected and limited to five gallons of diesel. Alcohol frowned upon. And machismo subordinated to seat belts and helmets.

Still, there are close calls. In 2001, the smallest entrant, *The Little Engine That Could,* was actually knocked onto its side, the driver luckily walking away unscathed. "One time I hit Schoesler so hard, it flipped me all the way forward," says Jerry Schuler. "If it hadn't been for my helmet, I'd've smashed my face on the steering wheel." He refers to six-term state representative Mark Schoesler, as of 2004 the only veteran of all Derby outings since the beginning. Schoesler, running for state senate that year, and two of whom would fit inside a Jerry Schuler outline, has won the grand prize four times in *Turtle* (think *Teenage Ninja*), a 1965 Massey model 92. He once also almost won a trip to the hospital. "I forgot to buckle the belt, and I took off and nailed Loomis—and almost went over the front."

"You don't have to be crazy to drive," says Mike Doyle, who's done it many times. He reconsiders. "Well . . . maybe a little bit crazy."

So, fun—of only a mildly demented sort. Indeed, the offhand attitudes of the senior competitors in this annual brouha could lead a casual observer to think they rate it merely ordinary on the scale of experience.

But then we come to 2002 Derby entrants Dennis Starring

and Josh Wills, athletic-looking, former Lind High football-playing cousins who balanced college with farm work and construction labor. Collectively, they owned and operated *Beaver Patrol*, a 1973 Gleaner model GH with a name just as politically incorrect as you think it is. Dennis's mother transmogrified the meaning by decorating the machine with a big, buck-toothed beaver face, complete with whiskers, and a flapping tail that comes off before the action starts.

These young men arguably personify the secret spirit that their more laid-back Derby-driving elders conceal. The danger? "It's a real rush." Are they normally risk takers? Seems so. "I'll drive anything," says Josh, "and push it to the limit."

"And we jump off cliffs," adds Dennis. Rappelling? "No, into the [Snake] river. Down by Lyons Ferry, 50–60 feet up. You have to wear shoes so you don't hurt your feet when you hit."

Youthful derring-do is not confined to Lind's male sector. Dawn Lobe, Leroy Watson's daughter who became a Seattle-area medical clinic manager, was at the helm of the women's combine that competed for six years. Photographs show her looking like a starlet, up on the combine, and she was an ardent battler. "My husband drove demolition cars, and the guys' girlfriends or wives would drive their cars in a powder puff circle race before the demolition event. And you were allowed to do some bumping. I'd get in trouble with him because I'd do a little too much, and mess up his car." How about on the combine? Nerves? "Oh, not really. A few butterflies, but the first hit took care of that. I wanted to win. I'd try to hit everyone. It's funner to go out there and hit than to dodge. It's more work trying to get away from the others."

Which would have been hard for her in any case. Carol Kelly, who crewed on that team ("I never drove, but I could have"), recalls that "Those men were such chauvinists. They really keyed in on her. They liked that there was a women's division, so that they could try to knock us out."

"Yeah," says Lobe, "they didn't take it easy on me." But she didn't take it easy on them, either. She became an accepted veteran, among those who'd typically pick someone in their heat to gang up on. "Mark Schoesler was a good one, 'cause he didn't like to hit so much." (Schoesler laughingly admits that the rule disqualifying drivers who don't make contact within three minutes "may have been written for me.")

"Of course, we usually took Best Decorated," recalls Lobe. And she won some heats, tied for another. But the combine itself proved fragile—once, the engine blew up, the transmission another time, breakdowns that the pit crew couldn't fix. In the end, says Lobe, "What was most fun for me was to go out there with a nicely decorated combine that was gotten together by women."

And as a true child of Lind, she'd keep on with it if she could. "Sure, if they had a combine for me to drive, I'd come back."

The idea of a resurgent women's team interested Captain Hook. "Hmm," he said, "I may have to try to organize that."

Which hasn't happened, but the gender divide definitely has been crossed. In the 2006 derby, Karlee Miller drove the resuscitated *Jaws*, while brother Matt and Josh Knodel entered another monster machine. And Karlee's younger sister Amy once again piloted an entry in the Derby's latest added diversion: grain truck races around the arena battleground during the breaks between combat heats.

If Carol Kelly, Bill Loomis, and their ilk in the Lions Club have anything to do with it, there will always be another year in Lind, and every year will be highlighted by the town's laugh-meter proof of survival, of unquenched spirit. Let the dust blow. Let the population further dwindle. Let even Mt. St. Helens erupt again. Come what may, by god, in early June there's still going to be a Demolition Derby. Folks will come from far and near. The combines will crash. The town will bulge, Slim's will bustle, the Golden Grain cafe and bar will stay open all night.

And the day after, the parade and the picnic. The winning combine and a few other survivors will join fire engines and antique cars and tractors—features of all parades around here— running very noisily up Main Street and out Rte. 21, applauded by viewers who've brought chairs for comfort. Then along past the park, where the barbecue is setting up, to the fairgrounds where the battle was held and some decrepit losers are still parked.

It'll be like old times, at least for a while—Lind, just carrying on.

But for how long? As the new century began, Lind had shrunk to less than half its high point of 800-plus residents. The high school's graduating class was down to six, and the prideful inter-scholastic sports program survived only by combining with the teams at former rival Ritzville High. Efforts to woo nearby siting of a new state prison came to naught, as did hopes for establish-ment of a top-shelf vodka distillery. "Lind is in trouble," said mayor Larry Koch, interviewed in 2006 by the *Ritzville-Adams County Journal*. There's no new housing being built, and "we're running out of tax base to operate our town with. Somewhere along the way we're going to need some way of getting money to run the town."

There are some positives in the picture. State grants helped to repave streets and sidewalks and upgrade the sewer system. Sur-prisingly, out of nowhere arrived Esther Ware, who had come into money, and with her grown daughters went looking for opportu-nities. She bought the Phillips block at a bargain rate, and set out to slowly refurbish its apartments and commercial spaces. In another unusual development, the Jacobsen family of Seattle bought

Lind's Methodist church building on eBay (10,000 square feet, $35,000) as the new home base for their online business, Birth and Baby Maternity and Nursing Supplies. The principal product of trade is nursing brassieres, in perhaps the nation's widest range of sizes and styles. Needless to say, the enterprise has become known locally as the Church of the Bra. Husband Jake commutes to his Seattle job as a marine surveyor while P. J., a lay midwife, and a lactation consultant active in the La Leche League, minds the fairly lucrative store. P.J. is aided by two sons who live at home, plus two locally hired staffers. The family also raises snakes, pythons included, for sale at reptile fairs. Some Lindites smilingly see "the Church of the Bra" harking back to the Garden of Eden, what with birth, breasts, and snakes. But the joking is mild, accepting. And it's a business with a truly beneficent purpose: "I want [breast feeding] to be a good experience for moms," says Jacobsen, quoted in the *Spokane Spokesman-Review*. She speaks from experience, having breast-fed her six children. "Women don't have to suffer. And babies have a right to breastmilk. That's what breasts are for."

Geri Loomis, one of the two employees, told the *Spokesman-Review* reporter that the business "gives this small community hope." But such unpredictable onsets offer no true future comfort. The main potential for the town still resides in the dedication of its residents.

As Myra Horton put it, "I'm sure something'll come along. We're just not going to dry up."

"People here," says Carol Kelly, "have the urge and need for this place to survive. We're just not going to sit back and let this town blow down the road like a tumbleweed."

Outside of Lind, the same gritty determination is evident at Bob Phillips's place (and rest in peace, Bob). In the 1960s, Hugh Phillips's sons opted for new technology, installing center-pivot irrigation systems on big spreads of their ground.[4] It's an expensive proposition, what with well drilling, pumping costs, equipment purchase, and maintenance. The new wells made possible a wide variety of crops, most notably including the high-value potato. But a large-scale venture into spuds sold on the open market resulted in terrific loss.[5]

In a kind of evolved historic continuity, much of the Phillips land moved into ownership by two of the newer immigrant groups: Ochoa Ag Unlimited, a corporate entity risen from the field work of Hispanic forebears; and the Hutterites, Germanic religiously communal farming people whose land acquisitions had moved in jumps from eastern Europe into western Canada, then down into Washington. (For more about both groups, see chapters 9 and 10.)

But not all was lost, A sizable amount of Bob Phillips's land remained in the ownership of his children. They continue cropping there, with a particular family twist. Bob's sister Mildred moved with her husband to northern California, where they developed a well-respected winery, marketing under the brand of R. H. Phillips. Her enterprise has reverberated on the home ground. Uphill out of Cunningham now, among the more traditional crops that irrigation supports, there's a plantation of wine grapes and a budding winery.

Santé!

6

They Feed in the Coulees

They feed in the coulees, they water in the draw
Their tails are all matted, their backs are all raw
Ride around the little dogies, ride around and slow
They're fiery and snuffy and rarin' to go

—traditional cowboy folk song

Let us step aside for the moment from the evolution of wheat farming and its communities to consider the mythically glamorized business of stock raising. Even though field crops dominate in Adams County's agricultural spectrum, cattle ranching here still comes in high on the list of market values. Herders of sheep and cattle were the first non-natives to establish themselves in this landscape, and their legacy is continually celebrated in the annual rodeos which, like NASCAR for mechanics, convert the skills of their craft into sport.

And that is indeed celebration, not memorial, because descendants of those original herders are still here, still ranching— over in the coulees on the east side of the county.

There we find Jake Harder and, among other creatures, his dogies. The name is traditional for calves weaned from their mothers, and Jake has a lot of them. But his are in much better shape than those in the old cowboy song.

Jake is a cattle rancher who could answer any casting call for the part. He's weathered and fit in his sixties, with a ready laugh and sardonic sense of humor, relaxed in work-worn jeans and boots on the March day in 2003 that I meet him. He and wife Joan and their two grown sons graze a herd of six hundred beef animals on a big swath of the scablands. For stockmen, this terrain was a gift from the great ice age floods: shallow, unfarm-able coulee bottom soils that grow natural forage. "Yup," says Jake, "The floods provided this place for livestock operations—it couldn't be plowed. Thank God for a few small favors."

Three Harder brothers emigrated from Germany in the 1880s and claimed land here. From the start they herded animals, con-tinuing their upbringing in Schlesweig-Holstein. Horses, at first, and then sheep as well. A lot of sheep. Some cattle always. But wheat? "Nah," says Jake, who cordially refers to his grain-grow-ing neighbors as "stubble jumpers." I remind him that a re-spected history of the territory noted an ancestral Jake Harder's planting of wheat in the early 1900s.[1] "Well, that was my Grand-father" he says, reconsidering, "and I tell you what, if you could make a penny, he probably did. As far as livestock, I don't think he ever had a herd of jackrabbits, but everything else: horses, sheep and cattle. He stuck right with it."

Whatever, because the money came in. Eventually, the Har-der brothers and their children assembled a vast stretch of land ranging north-south through three counties, one of the largest contiguous ranching operations in the entire country. Their de-scendants own it in portions. Jake and Joan's share is well up in the thousands of acres. Their homeplace is only twelve miles east of Ritzville, where the culture of grain manifests itself in huge trackside storage elevators. But those few eastbound miles transport you into the very different world of the stockmen who still reign in the county's toughest territory.

Getting to the Harders' place offers a taste of the way things were and somewhat still are in the continuation of that early enterprise. Turn off the county road through the break in the fence, vibrate across the cattle guard, and you're into the range-land that Jake's ancestors ran, and that—in modified form—their descendants still do. Cattle are standing or lying anywhere they please near the long entrance lane, making me nervous about which among them might choose to object to my car, or just lay claim to the road. Good that it's not nighttime: at least I can see them if they want to come check me out. I hit a deer once, a big buck with antlers, in the night up in the Colorado mountains, a creature I never saw until it ran out from the roadside trees and collided with my car. That was enough close encounter with big animals for me. But the cows are placid as I pass by, just casually looking me over.

Downslope then to the house built by Jake's father, where Jake and Joan raised their children, and where they still live. It's a nice place out of the sun in a grove of trees by Cow Creek, one of the few naturally flowing waterways in the county. There I meet Joan, a petite, pleasantly smiling woman who's heading out to a meeting of one of the several civic and professional organiza-tions in which she serves. She welcomes me with the news that Jake and son Cam (short for Cameron) will be home directly—they're out burning off some pasture. Sounds counter-produc-tive, but it's actually an adaptation of nature's own way (via lightning storms) to induce strong growth there next season.

Directly they do indeed return, arriving in a pickup truck—I had thought they might gallop up mounted—and we go in to talk. Again I find myself in counterpoint to the popular media's insistence that owners of large-scale agricultural enterprises must live in baronial estates. The Harders' home is an unostentatious, attractively comfortable dwelling, where the furnishings reflect the family's own choice and satisfaction rather than a style-minded need to impress. But there's one item that a movie director would have required: two holstered, long-barreled pistols with accompanying, coiled ammunition belts, casually parked on a table near the living room. And there are ashtrays, because Jake and Cam both smoke like chimneys.

Jake politely pardons the fact that I'm a novice in his world—I may have worked in the wheat, but never with cattle. He's genial, and informative—likes to talk about what he's doing, and the history of what he's doing, and it's a lively account. I learn that the first Harder settlers got their initial supply of horses from the Palouse Indians, then added more from the wild herds on the range. By 1895, the Harders had some 3,500 of those animals, which they sold to farmers and the army. They also drove as many as 900 at a time up to Alberta, Canada, for sale at a good profit. Particularly after internal combustion engines ended demand for the original horsepower, they owned immense herds of sheep. They and other local sheep ranchers drove bands of up to 1,500 of the woolly creatures more than one hundred miles to summer forage on the east slopes of the Cascades. The sheep had luscious feeding for a while on those better-watered slopes. Then it was back again to winter on the rain-refreshed meadows in the scablands.

Even as cattle began to be of greater interest, says Jake, "there were sheep run by my immediate family probably up until somewhere in the mid-1930s." But no more. Why? " Oh, sheep just don't cut it very well any more. Markets get real ugly in sheep. Labor costs are pretty high. And coyotes are a never-ending nightmare in the sheep business."

So it just kind of ended?

"Right. Although I had one experience with sheep. When they get loose, they *will* travel. There were some ewes came traveling through this country, sometime in the '60s. They were just traveling along about mid-February. So I saddled up my horse and went and gathered them up and brought them in. We just suddenly had this phenomenal little herd of sheep, and in four months the score was coyotes twenty-three, Jake nothin'. They just took them out."

There was one other factor in the decline of sheepherding: these animals eat their favored plants down literally to the nub, and this too-thorough feeding essentially wiped out the "ice cream" bunch grasses that famously nourished the early flocks.

So cattle came to predominate, in part, because they would eat whatever was left, even sagebrush. But knowing what's best for them, and where and when to find it on the range, is an important part of the knowledge developed by the Harder family's long ranching experience.

Russian thistle, for instance, which Russian-German emigrants unwittingly brought along from the Caucasus. It's the bane of wheat farmers when it invades their crops (it also becomes big tumbleweeds when dried out at season's end), but it's dessert for cows in its early stages. "When it's green," says Jake, "Russian thistle is delicious. Very high protein. Once it gets stickery, no way José. You can target . . . you want to get those cows there at just the right time, and they'll go in, and boy, you never see Russian thistle growing out on the range ground. Then there's some godawful stuff called fiddleneck tarweed. Have you ever walked out in a field late in the summer, and you've got little stickers all over, and by the time you're home they're in your shorts? That's fiddleneck tarweed. Once it's mature, you couldn't jam it down a cow's throat. But when it's green and growing, it's delicious. They just think it's wonderful. And kochia. You go down to Moses Lake in the summertime, and there's this big broadleaf thing growing out of the sidewalks. A cow will tear the fence down to get at that. They think it's the most wonderful stuff that ever happened."

And then there are the bad items, like Medusa head rye. "It comes up and it's got this spiney little seed pod on it and cows don't like to stick their nose down in that spiney stuff." And certain kinds of wild lupines "that a layman cannot tell the difference. You can have five lupine plants in a row and one of them will be toxic. And what it does, the cow eats too much of it and she kind of gets a little dopey and sleepy. If she eats way too much of it, it can kill her. If she is carrying a calf that is anywheres from 30th on to about the 80th/90th day of pregnancy, if she ingests too much of this stuff, it puts the fetus to sleep. That little rascal isn't moving around, he just lays there and when he's born he'll have front legs that are like this [indicating curled up]."

So the trick is to keep appropriate cows away from stands of toxic lupine during the crucial periods of their pregnancy. But there are some hazards that even careful herding can't avoid. Maureen Harder, formerly Jake's daughter-in-law, worked in the ranch's roundups, and recalls that the ash from the 1981 eruption of Mt. St. Helens became a peculiar and harsh food additive for the cattle. The ash filtered down like snow, piling up many inches deep in places, and it was tough stuff. It added good nutrients to the soil when farmers disked it into their fields. But the silica grit in it badly scoured and blunted the equipment used to do that, not to mention clogging air filters and other intake ports on engines. (And people who heard their roofs groaning under the weight of it lived in terror of rain until they could get it shoveled off).

It was truly a nasty accumulation. It coated everything, invading the mouths and nostrils of unwary people who didn't wear dust masks. The cattle, of course, had none of these, and most crucially had to nose into the fallen ash to find their forage. This rasping powder that could abrade steel farm machinery ground down the cows' teeth so badly that many had to be sent early to slaughter.

So ranchers and their creatures alike had to deal with this unwanted gift from the bowels of the earth. But Harder family territory also got some unusual extraterrestrial arrivals—at least, soon to be extraterrestrial. Seems that when NASA set out in the mid-1990s to design a wheeled robot for examining Mars, to be carried up there on the Pathfinder mission, they first wanted to test the little rover's capabilities down here at home. They dubbed their machine "Sojourner," and the focus of preparation for that part of Pathfinder's mission turned to eastern Washington's scablands.

Maureen, a junior high school science teacher at the time, recalls that "they thought the area on Mars where they were going to land it was similar to here, maybe even bigger." And close to home, some of the testing ground chosen was on the adjoining ranchland of Jake's cousin Herman. The family connection to this operation went further: Maureen was selected to join the group of teachers and students invited by NASA's public relations people to come along and observe Sojourner's tryout.

The Rover was a six-wheeled wonder about the size of a kid's toy wagon, chock full of sensors and radio gear, capable of speeds up to almost a blinding two feet per minute. But then, slow and steady wins the race, etc., and the Jet Propulsion Laboratory engineers who built it invented a suspension system of rotating joints that enabled its movement to "conform to the contour of the ground, providing the greatest degree of stability for traversing rocky, uneven surfaces."[2] In fact, it was designed to proceed while tilted as much as forty-five degrees as it climbed over obstacles.

Maureen and the other observers gave it a good workout, and they got one too: as part of the experiment, Sojourner climbed over some of the students themselves (it weighed only 24 pounds). But, mainly, they drove the rover. "We went to different surface areas—ash, rock, sand, loess, and gravel," says Maureen, "and we all got to drive it [think: the ultimate game joy stick]. And we all tried to get it stuck, but we couldn't."

Sojourner accordingly went to Mars, landing in early 1997, and once there indeed encountered surface material equivalent to powdery ash, plus lots of bare rock. And as it crept around, observing and sampling, it sent information to the teachers and students who had put it through its paces, telling them how much Mars really was like the scablands.

Meanwhile, Jake and family were continuing with their down-to-earth endeavors, the precise phases of herding: grouping their cattle by sex and age, moving them from place to place on their range. And they were, and still are, doing this the old way, on horseback—driving perhaps 150 cows at a time. Nor is there any use of Sojourner's terrestrial antecedents, the off-road vehicles and motorcycles that have become popular in some locales of the herding business.

"Crotch rockets? No," laughs Jake. "No, we don't use crotch rockets." The Harders keep a string of a dozen quarter horses instead. "A motorcycle doesn't have a brain, and those horses do. And boy do they get cagey. I mean, they really do get smart. You'll be moving a cow along, and pretty soon the cow'll start off . . . it takes that horse maybe two steps and he knows which way they're going. Those old horses that've been at this all their lives, sometimes they'll just move their heads and turn that cow back. They don't even take steps, just move their head."

But Jake and family are not practitioners of tradition just for tradition's sake. Take feeding, for instance. "We used to cut meadow ground for hay. We did that forever and ever. As a matter of fact, if you go back, the ranches that managed to stay together were the ones that had the natural meadows where they could cut hay to survive those nasty winters like in 1889. It's a different ball game as far as forage. I spent a great deal of my youth putting up hay. We don't do that any more. Back in the '70s I decided that I wasn't gonna be a slave to a damn hay bailer all summer long. Now there's alfalfa [to buy] everywhere, corn and milo, irrigation wells."

Nor do the Harders still raise their cattle to the full age for slaughter. They herd them through pasture with fodder added as necessary until the calves are weaned and competent. Then those animals are sent to a feedlot to fatten on grain and other prescribed comestibles. What about the prospect of consumer demand for a more "natural" beef product, fed by pasture grazing only? "The grass-fed thing is really a difficult game to play. There is no way that we can compete with Brazil or Argentina or Australia on grass-fed cattle. Our land laws are too damned tight." He's referring particularly to access restrictions that limit grazing on public rangelands to certain months of the year. And, of course, on his own land, natural forage is fine in the rain months, but shrivels in eastern Washington's dry, hot summers. "If you're going to offer a [grass-fed] product, then it's got to be available year 'round. So literally, there are many times, when corn is cheap and cattle are high, the biggest profit can be made feeding an animal corn. It is cheaper than putting him on pasture land, cheaper than grass."

That choice, though, can turn around to bite. "Everything is in the futures market—cattle, grain, everything. If the price of corn goes up, the price of cattle goes down. And who would ever guess that a few head of cattle with mad cow disease in Japan would have a crunching effect on the U.S. cattle industry?"

Tracking the trends of national and international commodities markets is just one measure of how ranching requirements have changed since the days of the truly open range. But there's other evidence that the Harders' operation is a model of modern stock raising: they sell their cattle on the internet. Don't bother looking for that website, however, unless you've got the right credentials: it's available only to people in the beef business. Laughing, Jake says, "You just don't want to put 278 steer calves on the internet and have two college kids drunk on Saturday afternoon order them up."

But selling on the internet isn't the Harders' only innovation in the cattle business. Jake has been recognized widely as an inventive expert in both ranching and range management. He's replaced windmills with solar cells to power pumps for water troughs. He has sent cattle to Colorado State University for market research, has even supplied a regional grocery chain's experiment in buying its own beef supply on the hoof. That didn't work out, principally because the beef market took a dive that year. But Jake, quoted in the somewhat fundamentally titled *Beef* magazine, said, "The idea has super potential for a small retail chain." In another edition of that magazine, he expressed his basic marketing philosophy: "Whatever works and whatever is right at the time, we'll do it."

So what about other New Age stuff, such as the growing demand for specialty meats, or bringing back that original western source of bovine protein, bison? Or even the back-to-the-future crossbreed, beefalo? Lean, native (or at least partly so)?

That, says Jake, falls in the category of *doesn't* work. "Beefalo are a built-in disaster from word one. The Canadian government did studies of those thirty years ago, and discovered they were never going to replace cattle. And buffalo, I can guarantee, will never replace cattle. The problem you get into with bison, well you'd have to have a hell of a deep pocket to ever get anywhere in the bison business. They'll eat grain, they'll do just fine on grain. I know a fellow that lives in Washington D.C., and he's a meat purveyor, and he'll go buy 150 bison, and put them up in a damn feed lot." But on the range there in the scablands? Would they eat the sagebrush, all the wild stuff out there?

"They'd do fine except they're just a miserable thing to deal with. You may've heard people say that you can't drive buffalo. Well you can drive buffalo . . . any place they want to go. I mean, they're kind of like herding cats, or alligators. It just doesn't work. They're basically a wild animal and they do not domesticate very well. They would just as soon stomp on you as anything else. They're big, and powerful, and some people think they're pretty smart. I don't think that a buffalo is very smart, he's just kind of a big bully, pushing his way around."

So into the foreseeable future, it's going to be Herefords and Hereford-Angus cross cattle on the Harder ranch?

"Yup," says Jake.

And looking to that future, what about the size of the Harder endeavor? The extended family's total holdings have expanded "pretty dramatically" over the years, Jake says, but he's not personally interested in a huge spread.

"You can't make a living with ten cows. And the way things are right now, you couldn't make a living with fifty thousand cows. Somewhere in between there's a set of cattle that you can manage properly. I've been to a lot of big ranches. The Deseret, down in Florida, I thought that was very well managed. But the time I was down at the King Ranch in Texas, I didn't think those people knew what page they were on, although I understand they've made some great strides forward. I've seen a lot of big ranches that were just total disasters. And they had nothing to do with the production of livestock. It was some industrialist that had megabucks and was trying to find some kind of an adequate shelter for vast income, and it was a hobby, and they just didn't get things done the way they're supposed to be done. You see that pretty regularly."

There's no chance of that kind of impersonal stewardship taking hold at Jake and Joan Harder's place. Both are actively involved in local service activities as well as ranchers' organizations. And you know they're thoroughly part of Ritzville-area society when you see Jake reciting Robert Service's "Ballad of Blasphemous Bill" to the Talent Show audience at the annual Wheatlands Fair, or playing a role in the annual community play, right up there along with his stubble-jumping neighbors. These are locally written, typically broad farces performed both at the Circle T Restaurant in town—dinner theater par excellence—and on the band shell stage at the fairgrounds, where people (and the crowds are substantial) bring their own chairs to sit on the watered green grass beneath the shading foliage of a double row of tall sycamore trees.

And where onstage dialogue stops whenever one of Burlington Northern's rolling noisemakers goes by—the audience reminded of the pause by Cub Scouts passing back and forth in front of the stage holding up signs that say "TRAIN."

Harders were here in the early days, and they're here now for the long haul ahead. I mentioned to Jake that, based on our interview, I could only assume that cattle ranching locally is an ongoing proposition.

"Yup," said Jake.

7

A Rose Grows in Ritzville

For the Harders and everyone else within a considerable distance, Ritzville used to be the closest thing to bright lights, big city. The Trading Company's department store, particularly, drew customers from all around. The Plagers' squeak-squawk runs up the coulee from Paha in their old Oakland were among many such excursions from all directions.

As the shrinkage of surrounding farms continued, though, and high-speed roads took hold, the ostensible city of Ritzville became what any truly urban outsider would call a small town. Not a tiny town, as Washtucna had become, or even smaller Hatton. Bigger than Lind.

But small. And, in truth, that's a good place on the register of American home places from which to look it over.

Small towns in literature and film tend to be conveniences: stage settings, mainly for either the goodness of cooperative simplicity, or compression zones, seething with tension—false fronts of cordiality shielding dark secrets that churn the repressed lives of local inhabitants. Grover's Corners or Peyton Place.

Ritzville, where population in the early 2000s had declined to fewer than 1,800 residents (from a high of 2,173 in 1960), falls somewhere in between—albeit on the high side of the neighborly scale. "You always give a wave to an oncoming car," says a local woman who drives in from her farm to work at the County Building, "because it's almost certain that you know whoever's in there." She also unworriedly leaves her keys in the ignition for her husband, in case he wants to transfer from his work truck to run errands. Other things unheard of in cities happen here too: bank tellers smilingly greet customers by name. Store clerks are friendly and helpful. And maybe it's only because there are so few people on the sidewalks, but you do naturally greet other pedestrians as you stroll along.

It's a place reminiscent of the William Inge drama and movie *Picnic*. There's a big municipal park, where children play on swings and seesaws under tall shade trees, and friendly gatherings at the picnic shelters share food while celebrating history and ongoing communality. Or consider the fairgrounds outside town, home to the annual Wheatlands Community Fair, where amidst cotton candy, ring toss, and traveling carnival rides, there's display of prize-winning vegetables, flowers, quilts, and baked goods, along with antique agricultural machinery. And kids from Future Farmers of America and the 4-H clubs bring forth the market animals they've raised as projects.

Heartwarming? Nostalgic? Indeed. But odd quirks poke through. Such as the Lung Lady, holding forth behind a table of gruesome wares at that same bucolic Fair. That's Public Health nurse Karen Potts, assigned for a while to an agriculturally-oriented version of the state's anti-tobacco campaign, targeted especially at teens. Her table of props includes two plaster teeth/ gums sets, one horribly discolored and diseased from dipping snuff (and beside it, an Andy Warhol-type model snuff can labeled "Dip-n-Decay"). Also: repugnant photographic display boards on lung and bladder cancer.

Most prominent are two sets of preserved pig lungs suspended from inflation nozzles (they travel with her from event to event in tupperware containers filled with formaldehyde). One pair of lungs is pink and healthy; the other is darkened and pitted from exposure to cigarette smoke. When Karen, grimacing (who wouldn't?) turns the pressure handle, the pink lungs inflate like balloons, while the porcine smoker's organs wimp miserably and leak air.

Lesson learned! (In another sector of the substance-abuse realm, there seems to be a fairly widespread belief that the only adults riding bicycles in Ritzville, and there aren't many, are people with drunk-driving convictions.)

And a television series featuring the town would likely emphasize such things as the local politico—responding to criticism from a prominent mortician—harrumphing "He'll never get his hands on my cold, dead body." Or the snooty attitudes of some older descendants of early settlers toward a newly arrived local businesswoman. And the temporarily suspicious fire that leveled the lumberyard owned by a dark-skinned Asian Indian family (it turned out to have been caused by an electrical malfunction, and they reopened across the street). That and the occasional appearance of yahoos sporting Confederate flags in the back of their pickups, or pasted on their bumpers.

As for me, I like to take a town's measure by its symptoms of disaffection. Graffiti, for instance. There's a solid sampling of it here, some artistic, some obscene, mostly just messy. But by unspoken agreement, it's confined to just one venue: the big railroad underpass out on Gun Club Road, a mile away from downtown. So much for teen rebellion. On the violent side of things, murder and rape are total rarities. In fact, reports of serious crime of any kind in the city, as noted in the weekly *Ritzville-Adams County Journal*'s Police log, are far outnumbered by complaints about loose pets, loud parties, and DUI vehicle stops—and even those are infrequent.

Really, it's an orderly city, on neutral ground as regards outbursting social drama. But boring? Not in the least. The populace here is far from uninteresting. There are many, of course, who fit the description of "ordinary citizens," no more nor less than folks you'd find in any town with its cheapest housing down near the railroad tracks and the well-to-do uphill: a range from miscreants to those pridefully sustaining their version of traditional local values.

But within that range, there are a number who classify as . . . unusual.

The Associate Jew, for instance, and the Associate Arab. And, of course, the man who built a real airplane inside his house, took it out section by section, assembled it, and flew away.

But let's start on the Bohemian side, with the Bowling Ball Lady, as she was identified to me by a hardware store clerk. That's Terri Cody, whose garden halfway up South Hill offers a fine, emphatic array of flowering plants within which are pyramidical piles of variously colored bowling balls. There's also a big stock watering trough. "That's the pool," she says. "I've had four people in there at once."

Cody is an émigré from the Seattle side of the state who, after divorce, evolved from waitressing to become a ceramics artist whose work is displayed and sold in many places around the nation. She doesn't use a potter's wheel, rather constructs her creations from rolled-out clay. When I visit, she's making some of her renowned, enigmatic conical women. Tom Waits, the gravelly-voiced iconoclast, is on the sound system. She's casual, with semi-short grey hair, red tank top, loose-leg tan shorts, and flip-flops. A small tattooed cat's head containing a yin/yang design displays on her right biceps—an indicator of the mystery she offers in explaining her choice of outdoor sculpture. "I just always wanted a bowling ball garden," she says, giving me one of her standard deflections. When local people ask why, she sometimes tells them, "So that you'll ask me that question."

Regarding her choice of this town for residence, she's more precise. "I wanted to be near a city, but not too near. I don't require much from a town. What I need is a library, a pharmacy, a movie theater, and a food store. My life is pretty simple."

Ritzville provides those amenities, although they've been made lonely in an urban place much reduced from its more glamorous days as a market center. East-west U.S. Highway 10 used to meet here with north-south U.S. 395, and traffic on these big-time routes poured through the business district. There were two hotels plus boardinghouses, and the block-square, two-storey brick edifice of the Ritzville Trading Company was the only department store anywhere in the region (and remained so well past midpoint of the 1900s). The city had twenty-two gas stations then, and five automobile dealerships. But Rte.10 was subsumed into Interstate 90, which joined the four-lane remake of 395 outside of town. The double bypass gave the city exit ramps, of course, but it became easy to speed right by. Result? Gas stations today, three; car dealerships, one. Chain motels and eateries (Starbucks, even) at the I-90 interchange up on the coulee's broad lip. At the same elevation, the blue water tower rises to landmark height above one of the town's advertised recreational attractions, the golf course. A bit farther down, there's another: a water park—swimming pool complete with water slides and other aqueous features. And just downhill across the street from the pool compound is the big leafy municipal park.

The welcoming sign at the freeway exit also recommends the city's historic center, down at the bottom of the coulee. The sloping decline that takes you there is like a descent through an archaeological revelation. It's the south end of town, and the newest houses, nearest the top, are ranch style from the second half of the 1900s. Midway along the slope, tree-shaded side streets reveal earlier and greater prosperity—big, Victorian-style mansions from wealthier days in the first half of the century.

I enjoy traversing these shady streets, seeing how the town grew and changed. And I've walked all of them. It's a very manageable pedestrian grid, as urban evolutions go—just ten streets north-south, most of them no more than fifteen blocks long, and only eighteen east-west, mainly seven blocks or fewer. There's just one traffic light—a blinker—at First and Division, the geographical center of the grid. Intersections away from the main streets have Yield signs rather than Stop.

When it is possible to walk a whole town, and feel drawn to so much of it, you enter into a kind of mutuality of possession with the place: because you have it pleasantly in the aesthetic fields of your brain, it also has you as a place you want to be. So it was, and is with me.

Near the bottom of that south slope, you come upon churches, among the city's oldest buildings. And on the coulee floor, railroad tracks parallel the three-street grid of downtown, with its brick-built canyon on Main Avenue, where continuity vies with change for attention. The Carnegie-funded library still actively ties down one end of Main's commercial zone. But almost next door, founder Philip Ritz's original hotel is vacant, near to collapse. Across the street, there's a new false front on a commercial building. Three combined bar/restaurants have neon signs out and—in spite of Karen Potts and her campaign—smokers now gather on the sidewalks outside or, in cold or rainy weather, fire up their cigs in retired small schoolbuses parked there for the purpose. These tobacco-loving clusters, never worrisome to pass-ersby, are the only signs of evening outdoor life downtown except for people walking to and from the movies.

The theater—the only one within fifty miles—lights its marquee for single showings Friday-Sunday. Controversial films are not to be seen there, and seldom anything rated as strong as PG. But going there for a show is truly a small-town experience: the wife of the owning family very pleasantly sells tickets—the small kind, from a roll—at the outdoor booth. She tears them in half herself. Inside, not a few of the seats are mended with tape. Audiences seldom fill more than half the place, but the show does go on, and praise be for that. The only other nighttime entertainment in town besides eating, boozing, and shooting pool, is the popular bowling alley, one storey of concrete plopped in where a former hotel burned down.

Withal, though, a bit of New Age has crept into town: there's a periodic farmers' market in season, for instance. More so, there's the annual summer Blues Fest, which draws renowned performers and big crowds to stages and food booths on blocked-off downtown streets.

Otherwise, visitors who aren't headed for government or professional offices are offered mainly expositions of the past. The history museum, for instance, in the decommissioned trackside Northern Pacific station (passenger service ended in 1969). An outdoor display of antiquated farming equipment. A parked caboose to remind of earlier railroad days.

And there's the railroad itself, a true presence. Train whistles—horns now, of course—are routine in Ritzville. No one here needs reminder of the Northern Pacific's evolution into the three-in-one Burlington Northern Santa Fe corporation. The amalgamated lines' thirty-five daily freight trains thundering through at literally all hours, plus Amtrak's daily Chicago–Portland/Seattle Empire Builder, north- and south-bound units both, keep the city current day and night with their warning blares for the five street crossings.

And those horns blat also as trains back and fill while loading at the big grain elevators—tall, round monoliths that dominate the skyline at the east end of town, rising high above surrounding rooftops and street trees. In the way that such things develop, they are owned by the evolved Ritzville Trading Company, which decades ago abandoned its department store.

In fact, this city survives as a place with urban amenities—limited as they are—mainly because it is the county seat. The governmental services offered in its late-1950s County Building breed both local employees and the lawyerly and other professional offices relating to government business. But Ritzville also has the regional hospital and a nursing home, increasingly important as farm owners grow older. It does have a scaled-down supermarket. And its airport—a half-mile airstrip, actually, with no control tower—is home to crop dusters as well as recreational flyers.

The spray planes, with their powerful engines, registered painfully with me. I lived not far from the airstrip. And when the dusters cranked up to take off in the morning, I wasn't sleeping any more. Incredibly loud.

But being near the airport was an attraction for my landlords, the Rambows, as I'll explain. That's Norm, in memoriam now, I'm sad to say, and Donnie. They once occupied a stately three-floor Victorian up on Nob Hill, a kind of mid-coulee geographical bulge that hosted the north side of the city's only challenge to the creep of wealth up the south slope. With their kids grown, though, the Rambows didn't need that much house. So they bought the former hospital, vacant after the medical folks moved uphill to a new facility. The old one-storey place had the potential for rehabilitation into apartments. But they didn't recruit tenants until later. There was creativity involved. The unusual interior space—aside from a comfortable converted living area in the former office and first ward—offered a combination of potential work rooms and a crucial long hallway perfect for building Norm's airplane. No joke. It was actually a glider equipped with an engine, but of operational size nonetheless, with a wingspan of twenty-seven-and-a-half feet—a project seemingly improbable unless you experienced the energy and joie de vivre of this couple: Norm, the creative, good-humored mechanic, and free-spirited Donnie, who buzzed around town in a blue Porsche decoratively painted with a checkered racing flag design. That was the car the Methodist preacher said told him by its noise that she was heading for church. (And when she put bells on her calf-high leather boots at Christmastime, he told her he heard them every time she crossed her legs).

The Rambows met in Kentucky during World War II. Norm, born in Millwood, near Spokane, had been intrigued by the thought of flying since he was a kid. So he enlisted to become a pilot. His training took him to Louisville, Kentucky, where he met Donnie one night on the street, watching a parade. He was of average height, and just one of many in uniform, of course, but his engaging expression—his face really preferred to smile—stood him out from his buddies. She was an office worker in a Reynolds metals factory, petite, dark-haired and pretty, "And he took ahold of my hand and wouldn't let it go!" But what with his training schedule and other complications, "We had a few dates, and then we just kind of drifted," she says. Until an only-in-Hollywood coincidence put them together for good.

Norm recalled: "There come up a guy asked me, he said I got a blind date and she wants a blind date for her friend. So I went, and there she was! And from that time on, we got pretty thick."

Norm was sent to the Pacific theater of action as a warrant-grade flight officer. He saw service in various aircraft all the way from the Philippines to Japan, most memorably and dangerously flying a small, unarmed L-5 over enemy territory. "I was marking the targets for the bombers. And I'd go right down to the ground and lay a smoke grenade where I wanted the bombs. But I was lucky. The airplane got hit lots of times, but not me."

On the ground, not so lucky. Norm came home with a Purple Heart for a shrapnel wound suffered when his unit's bivouac was shelled. And, of course, he returned with a pilot's desire to fly.

But that got put on hold for a while. He mustered out in 1946, and he and Donnie began an entrepreneurial career that eventually brought them to management of a filling station and garage in Ritzville—and finally, to ownership of their own garage. While Norm developed that enterprise, Donnie remembers that "Oh, I got into everything. We had a wonderful garden club. I was president of that a number of times. I was in Business and Professional Women, the Chamber of Commerce. The Fair Committee. Even on the Planning Commission for ten years."

Meanwhile, Norm's canny sense of possibilities (he installed Ritzville's first—and for a time, only—diesel tanks at his filling station) led him to focus on the automotive world's latest innovation: air-cooled German engines, and the Porsches and Volkswagens that used them. "I built up a Volkswagen repair business. And I was selling used Volkswagens as well, and I had quite a business going for a number of years, up until the time I crashed my airplane."

Just normal stuff for Adams County. Like Captain Hook getting shot for a deer.

"I was out flying, and I was over south, around Lind, and I saw this great big black cloud coming, and I knew what was going to happen. Pretty soon I got a boost, and I knew that it was blowing me. Well, as I got close to the field, of course I let down, and was coming down, and I was over the runway, and I had waaay more ground speed than what I wanted."

Norm cut off the engine to slow the plane, but that also cost him altitude. And he momentarily lost his grip on the control stick. "And I was close enough to the runway that I bottomed out. I collapsed the landing gear. Of course, when that happened, why, that was the end. I was sitting down! Had no cushion in my seat. And of course, my weight, all of it was right there, nothing to give but my backbone. And so that's what happened, I got crushed vertebrae."

He also got rods implanted in his spine, and his flying days were over. His pain-free days were over, too. But he never lost his sense of humor, nor the underlying enthusiasm with which he and Donnie confronted daily life. They moved north in retirement to the city of Spokane Valley. Norm died there in 2006, aged eighty-two, but has not left my memory. I only had to venture from the door of my apartment at the old hospital to think of his home-built wings and fuselage coming out of that building, and my admiration continues.

In retrospect, I still take intense pleasure from the indelible images imprinted during my daily ventures out from that old hospital apartment, into the town. When I turn onto Main Avenue to walk the few blocks to the business district, I try to imagine the scene ahead bustling with cars and people the way it was when the Rambows first came here, and the highway still went through Ritzville. But that's hard to do, because a kind of listlessness has settled on the city, a sense of suspension.

It particularly seems that way about eight o'clock of a summer morning, when I set out to get my newspaper. There's a vending box for the *Spokane Spokesman-Review* outside the Circle T restaurant, a long block-and-a-half along Main. It's the only downtown eatery open early, and there are always a few cars diagonal-parked in front. But the scene is otherwise deserted. The sun's bright slant angles big geometric black shadows onto the pavement from the houses across the street, creating a ser-rated, flat, anti-architecture that stretches ahead, increasingly emphatic as the business buildings rise up to three storeys and the shadows stretch farther. Bright house fronts, then bright brick canyon wall ahead on my side; dark suggestions on the other, huge round grain elevators looming up distantly where the buildings stop. The loudest sound is the slap of my sandals on the sidewalk. In the luminous, still morning, I am walking into a collaborative painting by Edward Hopper and Grant Wood, and I find that very satisfying.

Along the way, I pass a place truly redolent of the past. It's a two-storey white clapboard house with lower extensions to one side and the rear. It sits an amiable twenty-five feet or so back from the sidewalk, offering a low verandah in easy chatting range for passersby. The front yard sports two large shade trees, one of them a copiously productive cherry. It's the only house around that has a fence. And what a fence: a fetching, hip-high progression of inverted narrow iron-rod *U*'s and straight verti-cals, white paint chipping now, that tracks along the front and sides of the lot. Corner and intermediate posts are solid, cylin-drical iron, topped by very enticing finial balls—a bit roughened by the failing paint, but still cool, almost erotic spheres that attract and fill the palm. The gate features a modest French-curved topping. It latches via a strong spring strap of iron con-trolled by yet another, smaller ball, this one polished clean from long years of use. Grip the ball, the feeling of it the same as so many hands before have enjoyed, ease the strap out of its catch on the gatepost, and the gate opens inward to the narrow con-crete walkway. Swing it back to close—hinges complaining again with that reminiscent iron squeal—and hear a solid *klack* as the latching spring seats. Altogether satisfying to the hand, the eye, the ear.

And at one corner by the sidewalk, this barrier of utilitarian artwork supports the big rosebush that is my morning delight: a fine, lovely, spreading plant, its tallest whips as high as my shoulder and covered in season with velvety red blossoms, dark enough to show a hint of black. With no climbing support above the fence, it has reached up to its tipping point and widened into a thick fan of beautiful persistence. The Bowling Ball Lady excepted, Ritzville's home gardeners typically display only routine, orderly flower beds. But here at 310 Main Avenue, someone long before unleashed this resplendent, unkempt plant to speak for the house, and for a spirit in that house. And here, all these years later, it is still accomplishing its mission. Anyone passing by might think it strange to see me holding a blossom and speaking to the bush, but I am just saying: *You're gorgeous. Thank you.*

It is so dry here that on these morning walks, even if the temperature is heading for the high eighties and on up, the feeling of the air on my skin is fresh, light. When I walk farther on the same route later in the day, though, the heat is heavier, the hot air a more intrusive presence. Any exertion brings out sweat. But a jaunt along the four primary blocks of the business district is still one of the easiest ways to see what the area's shrinkage of population has done to local enterprise. Let alone that Ritzville Trading Company's full-range department store is long gone, the building so hugely vacant, many of the remaining commercial ventures that elsewhere would be stand-alone operations have had to be combined. Richard Grams, for instance, proprietor of R2J2, Inc., offers hunting, fishing, and camping gear, plus pizza and DVD rentals. Until recently, he also sold liquor, but transferred that license to the quilting store farther up the street.

Proprietor Stephanie White's Designer Carpets and Interiors also handles dry cleaning (which is done forty miles away in the regional box store center, Moses Lake) and UPS shipments. Ritzville Drug sells clothing, dishes, and outdoor furniture, and is a pickup point for FEDEX. The *Ritzville-Adams County Journal* vies with the drugstore in selling office supplies.

One of the more refreshingly idiosyncratic of the city's retail ventures ended when local historian and settler descendant Harland Eastwood closed his clock repair and antiques shop (home now to the aforementioned vending of quilts and liquor). John Rankin's Flying Arts Ranch, though, survives, down past the sheet-metal statue of Phillip Ritz, across the brick-paved town plaza from the Eagles' bar. Rankin, another transplant from coastal Washington, is an artist specializing in silk screen garments— and in hectoring the city and county governing bodies for better efforts toward developing and promoting retail commerce.

But my favorite among Main Avenue's stores, the Olive Branch, now closed, took first prize for variety of offerings. Proprietor Barry Boyer stocked an eclectic range of items, from serious antiques, unusual "collectibles," and used books to the current work of local artists: Terri Cody's ceramics, Linda Kubik's textiles, metalwork by Blowtorch Annie Smart, and Chris Clutter's photography, among others.

Behind Barry's cash counter was a serious display of model trains, as well as a framed presentation of his sleeve stripes and insignia from service in the navy. And in front of the counter he set out a half-circle of comfortable chairs for folks who wanted to sit and talk for a while—which Barry himself was fond of doing.

He formerly taught economics at a college on "the West Side," as the Pacific coastal plain is known here. Christine, his wife, is an investment broker. With children raised, they began a spiritual quest that led them to adopt principles of Judaism as guidance for their lives, although they did not formally convert to that religion (Barry smilingly describes himself as an "Associate Jew"). But they also wanted to free themselves from the living patterns of their West Side existence.

Barry had long wanted to move to the practical side of economics in the form of a commercial establishment. So since Ritzville had both a brokerage branch where Christine could work and available storefront space, not to mention reasonably priced housing, out they came. The name they chose for the store—Olive Branch—expressed their personal philosophy, as did the sign posted in the window: "Where Israel Stands, We Stand With Israel."

I sometimes tried to get a rise out of Barry about the small portrait of President George W. Bush he displayed, but he took no umbrage. He's a stocky, genial man with strong convictions. Among other things, the Boyers' sense of religious and social responsibility led them to adopt a young boy and girl from a Ukrainian orphanage, starting child-raising all over again.

Barry's full, graying beard and his preference for suspenders, neutral shirts, and dark pants caused some to wonder at first glance whether he might be one of Adams County's Anabaptist folk—a Hutterite, or failing that, a conservative Mennonite (more on these groups' presence in chapter 9). One among the curious was a Hutterite man who, despite learning it wasn't so, still dropped by to visit sometimes in the chair circle. That's where also one day I met Bill, a member of the Bahá'í Faith who laughingly called himself Barry's counterpart, an Associate Arab. And Dr. Miles Athey, a renowned environmental engineer specializing in indoor air quality management who has returned to his childhood homeplace while working on a formula for extracting fertilizer from seawater's brine.

Like the proverbial interchange around stoves at old-time

country stores, discussions at the Olive Branch ranged as widely as the orientations of the people participating. If the Bush portrait got mentioned, the political jibes and arguments that followed were of the good-natured sort that reflect foreknowledge that nobody's mind is going to be changed. Barry was avid, though, in his frustration about the decline of the downtown. Stores like his and the others selling elective items needed a flow of visitors on the sidewalks or at least cruising the street, scoping out possibilities. Like John Rankin, he thought the efforts of city and county officials and the Chamber of Commerce to lure traffic downtown from the freeways were uninspired and certainly ineffective, and he was politically active in trying to find better solutions. But in 2006 the negatives of Ritzville's commercial reality finally prevailed and he locked the door for good. The building stood vacant for well over a year until an outfit named Ritzville's Pretty Good Grocery moved in to compete with the small chain supermarket at the edge of town.

It's not that civic leaders haven't tried to find ways to stem the downslide of local commerce. The city promotes its water park, golf course, museums, and historic houses in a range of tourist-oriented venues, state-sponsored and otherwise. And in the realm of productive enterprises, state money helped rehabilitate a vacant downtown bank building to house a possible call center for perhaps a catalog sales company (although none had signed up by spring of 2008). Long-term hope for siting of a light industry park on the uphill outskirts continues, and the dream of a vodka distillery temporarily dropped its fairy dust in the same location. (Water supply for either would be problematic.) Unfortunately, plans are fading for commercial renovation of the abandoned old three-storey brick high school, home now to pigeons and vandals.

While it waits and hopes for some resurgence, the city is

pretty well reduced to its essentials—with that frosting of golf, swimming, chain eateries, and motels on top near the highway. Even as withering continues, if it does, the grain elevators, the hospital, and government and related professional offices, not to mention the bars and eateries, will sustain municipal life. Those, and the availability of Terri Cody's list of necessities: library, grocery store, pharmacy, and movie theater. Add banks and hardware. Plus, crucially, barber-beautician and undertaker—none of which exist elsewhere in the eastern two-thirds of the county.

As in Lind, though, the spirit of the community will be crucial in determining whether Ritzville keeps questing to flower again. As the new century's first decade advances, there still are leaders and activists with energy to keep up hope. Service clubs and church groups continue to take on civic responsibilities. The annual Blues Festival and the craft and farmers' markets give the city an image of youthfulness. And every year, the Wheatlands Fair—heavily dependent on volunteer work by Ritzvillians—refreshes the city's social, occupational, and cultural interconnection with the dispersal of farm families in this end of the county.

But Ritzville's population is aging, and with fewer farms around, there also are fewer farm retirees moving in to keep up traditional community activities, not to mention the tax base. The city will surely be here twenty, thirty years hence, but there's no clear forecast of how it will have changed.

I choose to think that it will be much the same. There'll be some new buildings, new jobs, and of course new faces, if only those of current babies grown up. But the city will still be hooked inextricably to the surrounding economy, even as the agricultural base of that economy evolves. Beyond that, the city will continue to take sustenance from its history. And the force of that history will keep an essence of Ritzville intact, regardless of changes.

On that score, the resilience of my beloved rosebush offers a positive omen. When I returned to Ritzville in spring of 2005, there were gaping holes in the house at 310 Main Avenue. And the rosebush had been savagely cut down. Seems the city had declared the house and its thigh-high front yard pasture to be hazards. The owner, enraged also by a disintegrating marriage, had weed-wacked everything and demolished the rosebush too, out of spite.

It lay where he had felled it, a sad pile of useless stems, shriveled flowers, and browning leaves, a complete disaster, a botanical corpse.

Time brought change, though, and renaissance. When I returned again in June of 2006, the wonderful fence was still there, but the house inside it had been demolished. Only its indentation remained at the end of the front walk.

But the rosebush had magically grown back up to its old size. It was, in fact, in full, ecstatic bloom.

8

Bringing in the Sheaves

We have harvest time here at present, and I am always enthused. I work even in the middle of the day in the full sunshine without any shadow at all in the wheat fields and I enjoy it like a cicada.

—Vincent Van Gogh

Van Gogh, of course, bespoke the intensity of color and texture that his increasingly fevered brain was converting to paintings. But the voluptuousness of a crop ready for cutting conveys itself also to the Adams farmers who reap this bounty they have grown from the earth. You can't avoid the esthetics of subtly undulating ripe wheat when you drive a combine through it for literally miles with nothing else to obstruct your view. Although the scene glosses into background the longer you keep at the mowing, the tones and substance of it are right there behind your eyes.

And while I have yet to meet a farmer who'd compare personal sensations at harvest to the sensibilities of Van Gogh's flying insect, I have encountered those whose satisfaction with the process certainly qualifies as a quiet joy.

Roger and Annie Smart, for instance. They farm some 2,300

acres out east of Lind, and their life there clearly gives them strong satisfactions.

They are an unusual couple, in that each has shifted focus to what the other set out to do. Roger grew up on the farm they now own, and went off to college to become an artist. Annie, from Montana, took up the study of agronomics. But then Roger came home to farm, the consuming demands of that work diverting his artistic bent to his photography. Meanwhile, Annie, having teamed up with Roger, added artistry to her farm work. Under the name "Blowtorch Annie," she shows and sells an intriguing variety of sculptures featuring such things as iron rebar twisted into graceful vines, and steel harrow disks torched to bring out subtle rainbows of color, then filled with water as birdbaths. She's also an accomplished musician, playing guitar and singing at church and at events such as the Combine Demolition Derby—for which she wrote (and recorded) the theme song.

The Smarts, children of the 1970s, are engaging and outgoing. Annie's short, dark hair sets off a face in which winsomeness and intelligence happily blend, conveying a lively interest in events both immediate and worldwide.

Roger shares that scope of absorption, as also Annie's joie de vivre—albeit in a less exuberant mode. His goatee and glasses would suit one of the stern, rigid farmers in Grant Wood's paintings, but his demeanor disqualifies him for that role: Roger's expression typically is of a calm, good humor that easily moves on to a smile or laughter.

Annie's work area for cutting, hammering, torching, and welding takes up one end of the big corrugated metal shop where Roger maintains and repairs the agricultural equipment. Like all competent farmers, he has to be something of a Renaissance man—able to fix almost anything that submits to carpentry, or wrenches, or the welding torch. But Roger carries agrarian multi-tasking a bit farther. In spring, for instance, this same guy who pulls out truck engines can sometimes be found out in his unfarmed conservation reserve ground, photographing wild blossoms—including the low-lying small ones he calls "belly flowers," those that make you sprawl flat in order to get a decent picture.

But it's harvest time now, and Roger is driving the farm's one combine in a field that begins not far from the house. He stops for me to ride along, and I climb up the side ladder to the door of the closed cab. There's an ostensible second seat in there, which actually is a backless cushion on top of a toolbox—a cushion that only partly blunts the rapid sharp jolting as the combine periodically moves across the rows instead of with them. The driver's chair by contrast is a throne, body-formed and air cushioned, reminiscent of an airline pilot's seat, what with the array of gauges and switches on the dashboard beneath the windshield.

There's a constant background vibration from the combine's engine and many moving parts, but the significant noise they make is amazingly hushed within the cab—silent enough that Roger can play the radio he's installed there. When I get in, he's listening to classical music, but switches it off to let us talk.

First, though, I've got to gawk. I've ridden in combines before, and as always the downward front view from the cab compels my attention until I get used to it. Just a few feet below, the wide, calmly turning header reel is endlessly, hypnotically bending wheat back to be cut by the advancing cutter bar. But in looking down I also notice interspersals among the grain of the lovely, slender, dark red grass named downy brome, contrasting prettily against the monochrome of the wheat. I ask Roger whether he sees his crop as with Van Gogh's eyes, and he jokes back "I hope not!" referring to the artist's mental disturbance. "And I've got both ears, too." But he goes on to talk admiringly about how Van Gogh made his own paints, and says he stands in awe of the man's original work—that reproductions don't do them justice.

And then he talks a bit about how his own eyes see the wheat, particularly when the new seed heads appear atop the still green stems, each head with its nimbus of hairlike extensions. "When those beards come out, in the late light the field turns to silver." And Roger was only partly joking at his alma mater when he told an inquiring student that his postgraduate artwork had evolved, that "I'm into stripes," referring to his equipment's markings on the soil. "Big stripes, and patterns."

In fact, when he's pulling the harrow behind his tractor, discing the soil in corduroy rows, he does sometimes make circles and other designs in the field. "We're about the most laid back farmers around," says Annie. "You've got to have some fun in life."

She's telling me this while at the wheel of the larger and newer of the Smarts' two grain trucks, this one capable of hauling nine tons of wheat. (The older, smaller truck is another of those aging stalwarts that seem almost ubiquitous around here. When I arrived today, Roger had one of its inside door panels off, fixing the window crank mechanism, grousing whimsically "you'd think these things would hold together better after twenty-five years.")

The Smarts' harvest crew this year consists of two young male friends who handle driving assignments, and a niece of Annie's from Montana who is a Jill of all trades. Among other things, this college student stays with the Smarts' bouncing young daughter Sophie while Annie drives out to the combine, loads up and heads for the elevator. She expertly works the gears and axle ranges as the truck labors through the soft soil and up out of the field onto the one-lane dirt road beside it. We soon reach a rudimentary, homemade traffic advisory marker called "the can," a rusty multi-gallon drum upside down on a fence post ahead of a sight-blocking curve. Annie hits the button on her walkie-talkie and says "Coming out!" The responding squawks tell her okay, the other truck will wait to come in.

And then we're off down the long, winding approach drive to the blacktop, and the five-mile run to the elevator. As we go along, we talk politics, and commiserate. The Smarts are among the relatively few registered Democrats in Adams County, but they are not at all alone in their distaste for the arrogance, elitism, and war policies of the Bush administration.

Later we sit on the verandah with drinks, talking leisurely as the day begins to cool. Sophie, a bundle of energy, cavorts on the green spread of lawn that fans out past flowerbeds and some of Annie's outdoor sculptures toward shade trees, the child herself a blossom in a floral play dress as she romps. At the table for dinner then, we hold hands in a circle while Annie asks a blessing for friends and food. And I find myself truly grateful for this day, my welcome into experiencing once again, however briefly, the elemental satisfaction of bringing in a harvest.

*   *   *

Roger Smart says that the 2,300 acres he and Annie farm, cropped half each time in alternate years, is about the minimum needed for a self-sustaining wheat operation in the drylands. Gretchen Borck agrees. She's the Issues Director of the Washington Association of Wheat Growers, with members spread across most of eastern Washington's counties, and some to the west. She knows of some farm families trying to make it with less land—and they are into hard times. "They have their wife working off the farm, for a reason: health insurance, point blank. And I have farmers telling me they haven't filed any income tax, because the tax return shows no income. Even with the wife's income, they still are in the hole. I have farmers who are saying, I'm going to get out next year, recoup what I can of my retirement. I don't think I have any equity left but I'll see what I can get, and I'll try to start up a second career. But it's not going to be farming."

Yet in Adams County, as late as 2005, the shakeout of farm failures appeared to be over, albeit for the time being. There were likely some families whose hopes would come under the hammer in years to come, but there was no sense of significant overturn in progress. The closest I came to Borck's description of a nonviable farm was—and there most likely were others I did not find—was the spread cropped by the Potts family, Karen, Steve, and their two daughters. And they were doing all right strictly on their own terms.

They cultivate one section of land—640 acres—inherited from Karen's Ferderer forebears, the main remnant of what once was viable acreage for family sustenance. They farm the ground, for their own satisfaction as well as the family economy. They've come back to Karen's homeplace because they didn't like the schools and other aspects of urban life in Spokane, where they first set up housekeeping. "Spokane's a nice place to live," says Steve, "if you like having a neighbor smack dab up against you. I never wanted to stay in a city—always wanted to be in the country." But he farms on weekends, when he's not working his trade as an electrician. And Karen is a full-time public health nurse, with a sometimes unusual job. As we saw in chapter 7, among other tasks of her profession, she's the "lung lady" who brought inflatable pig lungs from town to town to graphically display the dangerous impact of smoking.

But harvest is still a key part of this family's life, blended though it is with other priorities. And in that context it's clear that Van Gogh's happy cicada has landed at the Potts's place too, joining an array of other creatures in what amounts to a minor zoo. "We're involved with a pet rescuer," says Steve, "so we have like ten or twelve dogs, a burro, a couple of pygmy goats, and I have fish, and a boa constrictor, and my daughter has a snake, a ball python."

"The burro's like my dog," says Karen. "It's from an adopt-a-burro program, where they airlift them out of the Grand Canyon. When I was growing up, we'd have animals like chickens, and a couple of pigs, and I hated that. Because if it had a name, I'm not eating it. So we've got these tons of animals, they're totally useless. They're just here because we like them."

It's fair to say that the Potts's grain-growing endeavor is pretty much at the bottom of the size list of Adams County's wheat farms. Professionally, though, Karen's responsibilities connect directly with the top of that list. Her coworker and friend in the Public Health office is registered nurse Nancy Miller, who partners with her husband, Grant, in the operation of Miller Farms, third-largest among grain growers in the county. The cicada has landed at the Millers' place too—with a wide choice of landing strips on the roughly 13,000 acres of their enterprise—and has found there another family dedicated to both place and purpose.

Miller Farms has grown well past the point of need for family members to take outside jobs to keep the agricultural business going. But Nancy's professional skill and commitment propel her still into part-time work. (and most recently into election to the hospital's governing board). She and Grant have raised three children—Amy, Matt, and Karlee—all in college at the time of this writing (and all involved in the Combine Demolition Derby, as noted in chapter 5).

The family ties back to the wave of European settlers who came here early in the twentieth century: Grant's German grandfather was surnamed Mueller, but legally changed the spelling. Nancy, *nee* Pacheron, of Swiss extraction, came from Camden, north of Spokane. They met as students at Eastern Washington University, where Nancy graduated in nursing, Grant in agronomy. Then they made their home at the Miller family place some ten miles southeast of Lind.

Their two-storey house sits inside a high windbreak hedge atop a rounded knoll rising from a surrounding sea of rolling cropland. As at the Smarts and many other farmsteads here, there are no neighbors in view—even though that view reaches for miles. The questing eye settles instead on the back patio, the green grass lawn and the punctuating reds, oranges, and blues of the flower beds that surround the house. There's a picnic table, plus benches and chairs here and there for outdoor relaxation.

Inside, the house is spacious, hospitably and comfortably furnished, very much in keeping with the family's friendly, welcoming nature. Grant is cordial, a stocky, square-faced man with rimless glasses that distract from the sun-squint creases by his eyes. Nancy, as affable as her husband, is petite and fetching, with a nurse's competence showing in her demeanor and gestures. They are relaxed and jovial with each other.

Nancy, used to town living, found the isolated farmstead a bit daunting at first. But with her RN certificate, she was a shoo-in first at the Ritzville hospital, and then at public health. It was work by choice rather than necessity, integrated with her responsibilities at the farm. So she was able to take a multi-year sabbatical at home with the growing youngsters, and later return to her profession for just some days in the week.

But during harvest, as at the time of my visit in 2005, there's no part-time for anyone. Amy is driving a grain truck, Matt's operating a combine, and Nancy and Karlee are in charge of food for the crew. I'm soon to experience the delights of their culinary production, but first there is actual harvesting work to observe. And, as it turns out, to aid in a minor way.

Just as at Bob Phillips's place, we start with the combines resting at the corner of a wide-spreading, beige-ripe field. But this time I'm staying back as the big engines cough and power all that machinery into its work. I'm not totally useless, though. From time to time, Grant assigns me to move one or another of his vehicles to a new location. This time it's a grain truck, and walking the distance to reach it takes me sensorially all the way back to the Phillips harvest. The stubble I'm stepping through is closely spaced bunches of hollow straw maybe eight inches high, sharp enough at the top to scrape skin, but relatively brittle. It crunches under my boots, and the footing is queasy because the valleys between the rows can fool unwary ankles. The combined odor of the shorn wheat and the floury, cafe-au-lait tan dust that puffs up with each step slightly suggests the musk of old varnished floors, or antique furniture—a light brown smell, slightly acrid, but not unpleasant.

And when I reach the truck I discover that Miller Farms, for all it's efficiency and well-kept equipment, would be a target like so many other wheat growing operations if aged grain trucks ever decide to rebel. This one has a gearshift swing as wide as Montana and a boot-heel hole worn through the floorboard at the base of the accelerator. Later I learn that Grant sends one of his aged lorries every year for Amy to drive in the grain truck races that intersperse heats of the Demolition Derby.

My motorized jaunts are infrequent, though. Most of the time I'm standing or riding with Grant as the harvesting goes on. He is running only four of his five combines today. The fifth went home for repairs after being put out of service by a fairly scary accident while "roading" from yesterday's field to this. But watching him direct and supervise the progress of the remaining machines is truly to see a master at his craft.

His rolling command center is a small flatbed truck that carries a versatile mobile tool shop—the need for which is several times demonstrated in the course of the day. Combines have an amazing number of moving parts, and as work goes along, I become persuaded that Grant knows where each and every one of those items is located, and how to adjust, fix, or replace it. It's clearly a crucial skill, because during the morning three of the harvesters need repairs of one sort or another, and in each case Grant knows exactly what to do.

In fact, his diagnostic skills are remarkable. We're standing by his headquarters truck, the combines moving in echelon hundreds of yards away, when he suddenly points out at them and says, "He's got a clogged air filter. The number two combine there."

I'm astonished. "You can tell that from here?"

"Yeah, see the exhaust? It's burning too rich. And he was slowing down coming up the slope. We'll blow that out after lunch."

Primed to see a difference, I can barely make out that one machine's emissions—the exhausts rise vertically—are a bit blacker than the others, but I never would have noticed without prompting.

And later comes a kind of ultimate proof of this canny grain farmer's preparedness. One of the combines has stopped, and the driver radios that it is overheating, the belt turning his water pump is shot. Grant pulls forward the seat back of the headquarters truck, revealing an array of black rubber loops hung in the sequence of their numerical tags. "It's the one that ends in 02," he says, directing me to find and lift it off its hook, and sure enough, there it is. We motor out to the stalled harvester, where the driver has discovered that the real problem is a broken pulley, split down the middle, that has chewed up the belt.

Grant grins at me. "Now you're going to be really impressed," he says, and from the back of the truck pulls out the exact replacement needed for this one among so many pulleys on the machine.

I am indeed impressed, and continue to be so even after he explains that the same pulley had failed on another combine, and he had taken this from one of the elderly harvesters Matt is stripping for his Future Farmers of America project—a functioning business named Matt Miller's Used Combine Parts.

"This thing costs $45.00 new," he says, brandishing the replacement, "and I think they got a bad batch of them [at the dealership]. Those people who make these, they don't give a damn what happens out here."

But the injured pulley is seated in a very inconvenient place, near enough to the hot engine to guarantee burns for probing hands. And it's almost noon. "Well," says Grant, adding another repair to the afternoon list, "we'll let it cool down over lunch, then get a wrench in there."

And so we move from the heat-fevered landscape of Van Gogh to the softer palette of Monet and his impressionist contemporaries. The meal is laid out on a table in the tree-shaded yard of a nearby farmhouse that came along with the deal when the Millers bought its acreage. Its occupants are away for the moment The toilet within is quite welcome, and Nancy and Karlee have stashed towels by the outdoor tap for the muddy, much needed splashes of washing up. They've also brought a huge platter of sandwiches, plus crudités, pitchers of cold lemonade and iced tea, and fine cookies.

The younger members of the crew luxuriate down on the

grass, while the older guys, like me, take advantage of lawn chairs. There I learn that I'm not alone in my affection for harvest work as a temporary pastime. One of the truck drivers is Nancy's uncle, Clay Smith, a retired college administrator. And Ritzville police chief Dave McCormick is doing his annual stint driving a combine in the Miller harvest, which he clearly loves to do. His machine is decorated with a decal of the town cops' shoulder patch, and is known as the official police combine.

Conversation eases down to restfulness. The cool green of it all, punctuated by flowers, blessed by the calm silent absence of engines, is a fine lull. And again I am captivated, feeling the happy sense of immersion in a process descended from time out of mind, this modern-day version of bringing in the sheaves.

* * *

Of course, it's easy for me to take such outsider's enjoyment, dropping in just for the finale as I've done. But it's a satisfying time for the farm families also (unless their crop is poor), and likewise for the farming community, which traditionally commemorates it with harvest balls and celebrations. And, of course, it's a relief—the culmination of a year's demanding sequence of episodic labor, interspersed by worries about hail, rainfall, lightning, weeds, pests, blight, operating costs and what the markets are doing to prices.

Dryland wheat farmers typically work their acreage nine or ten times a year—cultivating, fertilizing, weeding, seeding, spraying, harvesting. And depending on what equipment they're using— tractor pulling any of several implements, or running the trucks and combines—they can tell you the expense per acre for that work. There's an important equation hovering over their efforts: any profit for the year will be a factor of total bushels harvested times market price per bushel plus government support pay-

ments, minus outlay for seed, fertilizer, chemicals, fuel, maintenance, crop storage, insurance, loan interest, and family expenses.
Budgeting becomes particularly dicey when there's volatile upward pressure on major cost components, particularly petroleum,
which is basic to fertilizer as well as fuel.

And there are two big catches in the situation. First, expenses
continue around the year, but income from government payments and harvest arrives only in widely spaced periodic doses.
So there's a rolling, symbiotic relationship between farming and
banking, with annual loans simply a factor of life either for this
year's operating costs or preparation for the next crop.

Second, the market for wheat (as for most agricultural commodities) suffers fluctuations completely beyond growers' control. A bad crop in the Midwest, say, or in any of the world's
grain importing countries, increases demand for Washington's
wheat, and sends prices up. Bumper crops in those locales have
the opposite effect. And riding herd on prices even in the best of
times are the grain industry's huge merchant corporations, Car-
gill, Archer Daniels Midland, and others whose market domi-
nance effectively redefines and compresses the hallowed inter-
play of supply and demand.

That corporate pressure is not new among the forces driving
farmers' calculations of their livelihoods—nor in the purchasing
lives of consumers either. The profit plans of the businesses that
ship and sell harvests, and others that process the raw products
into food, impose themselves powerfully on those who produce
those products in the first place. It was the blatant profiteering of
the crop-hauling railroads that spurred development of early
pressure groups such as the National Grange, and generated the
federal Interstate Commerce Act and its federal operating Commission in 1887. Even that proved insufficient protection, however, and the more politically focused National Farmers Union

and the American Farm Bureau Federation emerged to join the Grange in action. Their battles to win better market control for small- and middle-scale farming operations, although politically successful, have been substantially outflanked by the oligopolistic evolution of the commodity marketing and food processing industries, and the resulting, adaptive increase of large-scale corporate agriculture. Even in dry wheat country, where big-time corporate control of farming has not taken hold on the ground, the relentless treadmill of technological advance, pushing costs always up for more effective machinery and chemicals, has brought home the mantra of modern American agriculture: *get big, or get out.*

The consequences are stark. Like two barometers beside each other, one of them upside down, the average acreage of our country's individual farms has risen, as has total acreage of land in farms, while the number of those farms has fallen. The agricultural population also is on the falling side, both in numbers and in proportion of the body politic: In 1900, farm residents were 42 percent of the American census. In 2006, they're less than one percent. Yet because of technological advances, the amount of food and fiber produced by this condensing sector of our citizenry has exponentially increased.

It's a pattern of change inseparably intertwined with the corporate centralization of Americas food business, and government's encouragement of that process. In much of Europe, the cultural tradition and continued presence of rural towns and family farming has won political protection. In the United States, after big money recovered from the Great Depression of the 1930s and began to attack the Roosevelt era's protections, things moved in the other direction.

Congress' ongoing policy of subsidizing food costs for the public has both encouraged and comforted the emergence of enormous cartels, vertical integrations of large-scale producers, processors and marketers of agricultural commodities, often combined under a single corporate roof. Notably, as profit demands at the top of these corporate pyramids undercut the goal of cheap consumer comestibles, it's the remaining independent farmers who make up the difference by earning less for their crops. An old but accurate aphorism tags farming as the only business that sells wholesale and buys retail.

The balance in that equation has always been dicey—and has always been at the not-so-tender mercy of those who handle crops after farmers have grown them. It's been a seesaw battle in which Congress has for decades sought ways to give stop-loss protection to independent growers—whose numbers, even in decline, still exert powerful influence in rural electoral districts—while simultaneously comforting the profit margins of expanding agribusiness' corporate boardrooms.

The outcome on the farm side—at least for internationally traded crops including wheat, corn, soybeans, and cotton—is a complex array of guaranteed and optional government payments that make up the difference if commodity market prices drop below a formulaic threshold. These supports also offer options farmers must choose among for how best to maximize payment for harvests. There are also crop insurance and loan guarantee programs tailored to the annual agricultural cycle. These "incentivizing" measures, as one USDA operative terms them (the word *subsidy* is not politically favored), are designed "to yield income stabilization to rural America, and price stabilization to consumers."

On the first count, one is tempted to say "too little, too late," and the second surely depends on who's doing the shopping. But both Roger Smart, at the smaller end of the dryland farming success scale, and Grant Miller, at the larger, assert the importance of all these modes of assistance to independent wheat growers. Yet it's a partly conflicted endorsement, because one element of this array gets blame as a principal latter-day cause for the decline of rural towns.

That's the Conservation Reserve Program (CRP), which pays farmers a stipend for every approved acre (especially those on ground that's only marginally useful) that they plant in non-commercial, soil-holding grasses and shrubs. Grant Miller particularly agrees with those who believe that CRP ("the grass," as it's sometimes called) may be preserving soil, but has contributed heavily to civic erosion. Up to 25 percent of an agricultural county's arable land can qualify and Adams County (like many other counties around the country) has hit that limit. "You take that much ground out of production," says Grant, "and you'd better bet that puts a crimp in demand for goods and services from the farm sector."

CRP has also generated obloquy and derision among urbanites: *You're going to pay them not to grow food? Soft life!*

That vexes Roger Smart. "Look," he says, "that's just backward. In fact, it's the government leasing my land for the purpose of conservation."

Grant agrees only to the extent that land going into CRP is highly erodible, or in "buffer zones around streams and rainfall runoff channels, you know, to keep soil from ending up in Portland or Astoria, out on the coast." But he believes the program's acceptance of enormous amounts of good acreage, especially whole farms, revealed a deeper purpose: "Lowering supply. Nationally. They took out thirty-six million acres of wheat. They just labeled it conservation so it would pass through the house and senate."

Of course, that was in 1987, and as Roger points out, if the intent of reducing supply was to boost prices by intensifying demand, the result was not great. Both growers agree, however, that steady CRP payments are important to farm budgets, those being so vulnerable to market shifts. And they find common ground also in objecting to the current national administration's attitude toward family farms. "That's who Bush is hurting now with the farm programs," says Grant. "They've cut back, believe it or not, even though all the red states voted for him. Cut and cut and cut." If payment reductions go too far, he says, Miller Farms would be sustained by its large spread of ground. "We'd survive. But somebody's got a farm of one thousand acres won't. And that's not good. It really isn't."

On a fine evening in mid-June, though, such considerations are secondary to sociability as the Smarts and a crowd of other Lind-area growers and their kids gather for beer, soda, barbecue, and buffet at the Millers' home. It's the end of the day of the Combine Demolition Derby, and the congenial, easy-going mood of the party bespeaks a true sense of community. Not just silent pride at being so competently able to pull off the day's large-scale, zany event. There's also an unspoken but palpable mutual satisfaction from sharing the creative, successful function of growing grain. These are the folks who can do it, and do it well.

An unusual pelting shower of rain had drenched the Derby audience at the end of the event. But it also left the air fresh and cool as it moved away. Now the broken remnants of storm clouds are exclamations of sunset in the fading blue of the western sky. As deepening dusk increasingly isolates the lighted conviviality atop the Millers' knoll, it seems that a sense of contentment has settled on the land.

9

In the Land of the Potato

The potato has: humbled Spanish conquistadors in Peru (in the 1500s); befuddled cooks employed by European royalty (in the 1600s); so impressed Marie Antoinette that she wore its buds as hair ornamentation (in the 1700s); brought ruin to Ireland (in the 1800s); and developed into a multimillion-dollar industry in the United States (in the 1900s).

—Jacket blurb for *The Amazing Potato,* by Milton Meltzer

Time to step back for perspective. There's more on the major menu in Adams County than wheat and beef, although their agriculture occupies most of the land. Due to latter-day developments, as we'll see, lesser crops have emerged in the west end of the county—legumes, alfalfa, corn, even some fruit. But champion among these newcomers, rising in fact to the top in economic importance above even grain and cattle, is South America's native tuber, the potato.

In the realm of edible things, this plant really does have an amazing history, although not quite so instrumental as the blurb above would indicate.

It was actually a potato *sickness*, for instance—the blight— that brought ruination to Ireland. And that only happened because the deprivations of the British penal code and corn laws had made spuds so crucial.

Yet it does seem to be true that wherever these bulbous items are farmed, they gain social importance far beyond what their lumpy dowdiness would seemingly merit. That's certainly the case in Adams County, which grows and produces fully half the United States' supply of french fries. Potatoes are now the biggest cash crop in Adams, where this unassuming vegetable has spurred a new wave of immigration, and has helped give rebirth to what's now the county's largest city—Othello.

We'll get to that name in a minute.

Potatoes came to their prominence in Adams not solely on their own merits, but because of background forces—in this case, the onset of water. Irrigation. The tubers are grown especially in the thick panhandle that juts westward from the lower left corner of the county. This is Adams's driest territory, averaging less than ten inches of yearly precipitation. It is both lowest in elevation and closest to the rising Cascades, and thus deepest in those mountains' rain shadow. And it's a place plagued by one of the weather gods' worst tricks, called *virga*—precipitation in hot weather that evaporates before hitting the ground. Desperate farmers lured here by good rain years in the early 1900s soon were paying so-called "rainmakers" to fire chemical cannons at whatever clouds showed up.

But nothing worked until canals opened in midcentury from the Columbia Basin Irrigation Project, waterways tracking southward seventy-five miles and more from the reservoir formed by a premier feature of Franklin Roosevelt's New Deal—the great Grand Coulee Dam, out west of Spokane on the Columbia River. These long, wide ditches brought water only to the western half of the panhandle. But surviving farmers in much of the unwatered remainder took advantage of farming technology's latest development: center-pivot irrigation systems that pumped the fluid up from underground aquifers. As earlier noted, these amazingly ungainly but effective, stretched-out, flexible lines of motor-wheeled sprinkler pipe, almost a quarter-mile long, propel themselves slowly around a well head. They create the big farming circles visible in satellite photographs, let alone the downward views of airline passengers.

With all this new water, harvests previously unimaginable on such dry ground began to flourish: alfalfa hay, bluegrass (for seed), kale, clover; lima beans, dry beans, and even sweet corn. New crops suitable for delayed marketing brought food processors with their giant packing plants. At first sugar beets took the cash prize among the new harvests, but the demise of that market left potatoes the eventual champion. And as the need for labor in the irrigated fields and new food factories pulled in a new working population, Othello, in the heart of the once-dry panhandle, shrunken by failing fortunes, was revivified, transmogrified.

New bodies were needed for the evolving economy. But, locally, there were none to spare. The numbers of original Euro-American settlers and their progeny had shrunk in the dry times, and railroad work, once a solid municipal sustenance, had withered, the families gone who had depended on it. But the dynamic of immigration, the magnetism of available wages, did not fail. The town began to grow, and then continued to bulge, absorbing the latest successive wave of outsiders seeking a measure of prosperity.

This time, the new blood was largely Mexican.

* * *

I went to Othello expecting to find some public celebration of its precocious name: a replica of Shakespeare's favorite Globe Theater, perhaps, or a statue of the Black Prince—at least some prideful historical connection such as one finds in the town of Odessa, northward in Lincoln County. There, the geographic Russian-German reference is front and center in the annual Deutchesfest, with beer awash, oompah bands performing, and all manner of Germanic foods for sale.

But in Othello? None such. Like Lind, this city has no certifiable explanation for its name. The best guess is that the christening was simply the personal preference of an early postmistress who seriously admired Shakespeare. Regardless, the reference has not reverberated. Aside from a set of minor streets named Desdemona, Macbeth, and Venice, the city simply ignores its nominal relationship with the Bard of Avon.

In fact, for several decades it was better known for its connection to Wisconsin. Othello wasn't chartered until 1910, making it the youngest of Adams's principal towns. But in 1908, the Chicago, Milwaukee & St. Paul Railroad built through on its line to the Pacific. The city became a division headquarters for the Milwaukee Road, as that outfit was commonly known, and rail-related business boomed while the farmers roundabout struggled to survive. Most of the town's 300-plus residents until the 1940s were railroad people. Then, in a kind of serendipitous duet, failing sustenance from the railroad coincided with the onset of water and the rising economy of food. The Milwaukee Road ceased passenger service in 1961, went into bankruptcy in the '70s, and in 1980, as also in Lind (see chapter 5), literally pulled up its trackage, demolished its stations, and disappeared.

But canneries moved in, and fertilizer plants. And 1961 saw the arrival of the first frozen food processors. Three years later, Chef Ready brands began the vastly fateful production of frozen french fries.

So, the baton was passed. But the transition was not a thing of beauty. Via fire, demolition, and an absence of planning, Othello's physical civic history went down the tubes. Only two small original commercial buildings remain, almost hidden. Not here the proud, if deteriorating, brick eminences of Ritzville. Instead, there's a helter-skelter of latter-day low-rise concrete, poured with little imagination, bringing to mind writer Gertrude Stein's epithet about her California hometown: "There's no there there."[1]

Remember that the basic mapping of land around here is in mile-square sections, drawn with neat compass boundaries. Othello occupies two of these, joined as a block north to south, with a bit more of two neighboring sections attached on the sides.

The contents of the city lie roughly in east-west bands across this grid, with First Avenue, a kind of surrogate main street, making a catch-as-catch can belt in the middle. Banks and restaurants, a government center and the few motels, some of them graced by trees and irrigated lawns, are spaced apart among nondescript buildings along this mile. The small streets running parallel on either side sport a hard-to-sort jumble of government and business structures.

Flat streets of neat, green-yarded mid-twentieth-century houses spread away in square blocks on both sides from this central belt. No showy homes, no Ritzville-style big Victorians here. These neighborhoods end, on the north, where farming begins, and on the south, along State Route 26, where big storage structures for crops and fertilizer loom up, interspersed among the block-long pipe- and tank-bestudded canneries and freezer plants.

What's closest to a heart in this city has no buildings at all. It's parkland, running for a third of a mile just a block north of First Avenue, a zone of green grass and trees, sports fields and picnic areas, a downsized version of New York's Central Park.

This big stretch of greensward gives evidence both of the city's continuity, and its evolution. Here, just as in Ritzville and Lind, the original settlers who dug their wherewithal out of hot dusty acres gave themselves civic leeway to create luxuriant communal space in which to relax. They would be astonished now (and, in truth, some of their descendants—the few who remain—still are incredulous) to find that the soccer players on the sports fields and the picnicking families mainly are Hispanic.

But the fact is that this latest influx of non-native people is simply a continuation, a repetition of the process that also brought those earlier settlers here.

Emigration is a push-pull proposition. Nobody says well, gee, things are great here at home, so I guess we should pick up and make a miserable hard trip for thousands of miles and take our chances in a new place where the situation is really questionable. Usually, it's a combination of necessity and hope: difficulty in one place, opportunity—either actual or imagined—in another.

So the rise and retreat of hard times around the world tends to cause surges and slackenings of expatriation. The potato famine in 1840s Ireland set off a great migration to the United States, where booming industrialization was sucking in unskilled labor. Germans in that era left home for American farms and factories because of persistent European warfare. Impoverished peasants in China crossed the Pacific for the Gold Rush and the building of America's railroads. And Russian Germans came because they were sandbagged by a new Tsar.

These were Germanic farming people wooed to resettlement in the Crimea and lower Volga River territory, north of Turkey, by Catherine the Great of Russia. She gave them land, intending that they should teach her subjects in that relatively dry place how to prosper in agriculture. Importantly also, she allowed the émigré Germans to govern themselves and keep their language, and excused them from military service. But a successor, Czar Alexander II, rescinded those exemptions in the mid-1800s. The prospect of army conscription was a real threat to men of almost all ages in that era of European strife, and a particular burden on those who were Mennonites and Hutterites,"quietist" Christians who forswear any military activity. Into this uncertain scene in the 1870s came advertisements and salesmen for the new American railroads, recruiting settlers for their government-granted lands. Many families, Lutheran, Mennonite and Hutterite alike, pulled up stakes again. Those who eventually came to eastern Washington brought with them a variety of winter wheat, from the Caucasus region, known in this country as "Turkey Red," a grain well adapted to arid climate. It's designated a hard wheat, and it mills well for bread and rolls. As things turned out, it was Turkey Red that enabled early wheat farming to survive in Adams County. When the truly dry years pressed down, Turkey Red was almost alone in yielding enough cash to keep farmers in business.

But it was other crops, the watered crops, that brought Mexicans to Adams and eastern Washington. And true to the global pattern, they came in surges at different times from different parts of that country, and in different sets of circumstances.

The experience of Al Ochoa's family, for instance, fits the same hopscotch paradigm of the Russian Germans, albeit on a different travel map. "They emigrated from Spain to Chihuahua state in Mexico," says Al, who after several generations became the chief of a very successful corporate family farming enterprise. "And then there was the revolution there, so they moved up to Texas, and ended up in Colorado. In 1939, my grandfather came over here as a migrant laborer to work in the sugar beets in the Yakima valley," which is two counties west of Adams, across the Columbia. "They liked his work so much they invited him back."

And the family liked the area well enough that they stayed. The ancestral Ochoas moved to Othello in 1958, when irrigation had spurred cropping of both sugar beets and potatoes in the Adams panhandle. By 1965, they were on their own land near Mesa, across the line south in Franklin County, but still in the zone of the new irrigation. Al met his future wife, Diane, in the Mesa high school. He worked his own first thirty acres there in 1973. And then it was upward and outward to a spread of farms run by members of the extended Ochoa family within the coordinating structure of Ochoa Ag Unlimited, with Al at its center. The Ochoas were not only among the earliest Hispanic immigrants to eastern Washington, they were—and are—among the few who became substantial landowners. For most who came later, the increase in both the cost of land—particularly irrigated land—and the equipment needed to farm it made other paths to success more viable for most newcomers. Homesteading was a thing of the past.

"See, there've been three waves of Mexican immigrants," says Frank Martinez, an affable, burly potato grower. Smiles and earnestness soften his strong face. "First wave, it was only the exceptions like the Ochoas who came here, and it was mostly in the 1940s. People then came up mainly from just below the border, and only a few made it to here. Most worked the fields in Texas and Florida. Then there was a second wave, starting in the 1950s, from farther south, including my people. And the third was in the late '80s, from far south in Mexico. They're the ones doing the field work now."

That continuing third wave—call it a tide, perhaps, so great a concern it has become in American politics—is propelled largely by the economic devastation wrought on Mexico's small farms and wage-labor work force by the impact of the North American Free Trade Agreement. NAFTA's supposed spur to Mexico's economy worked only for large-scale agriculture that could compete with subsidized commodities from the United States, and for border-hugging Maquiladora factories and assembly plants paying wages low enough to fit within the profit structure of the American corporations they supply.

Even menial labor in the United States pays enough by comparison to prompt the onerous journey northward from home. And while field labor can be menial indeed, in the mechanized world of so much of American agriculture it can offer a step up in income. That, and the entry-level jobs in the processing plants. Still, the graduation for these newest arrivals into the residential stability achieved by many before them will take longer—particularly since, increasingly, the emigrants of this third wave have brought some of the social pathologies of poverty to their new locations, although less so than in more crowded urban places. And the range of their potential paths upward has been limited by the immense cost now of land and equipment to begin farming; mechanization's depletion of mid-high-range factory jobs; and the de-skilling of America's other evolving labor requirements.

The process was better for the second wave. That was the surge which brought the first significant numbers of Latino settlers to Adams County, as elsewhere in the Pacific Northwest. Many descendants of those emigrants are now in the professional and entrepreneurial sectors of local society. Olivia Vela, *nee* Escamilla, for instance, manager of one of Othello's main commercial bank branches. Her parents, who owned a farm in Mexico but still needed income from migrant farm labor, crossed first into Texas. Her father's work in sugar beets brought them to eastern Washington, where they settled in the 1960s. Olivia was born in nearby Moses Lake. Her husband, whose family's track northward is similar to Olivia's (although his parents have retired back to

Mexico) is a medical worker. Mexican names are prominent among the city's lawyers. Police officers. Realtors and restauranteurs. Notably also, several local Mexican families operate prosperous trucking businesses for the agricultural trade.

Frank Martinez, however, has risen to the top in agriculture itself, without having to become a farmland owner. The money markets opened by irrigated potatoes also created a niche for growers who invest in the expensive equipment needed to farm the spuds. The thing is, irrigation makes crops grow so well that you can't keep on growing them year after year—they use the soil chemicals differently, their viruses linger, and so forth. On dryland, you can grow wheat every other year because the land (aided by fertilizers and herbicides, of course) is receptive again after a fallow year.

But it takes at least three, or more commonly, four years for sprinkled ground to be ready for potatoes again—time for the soil chemistry to recover, and for hostile organisms to wither. So potato growers like Frank rent the use of irrigated circles only as they come available for a new crop of spuds. Their investment—Frank's investment—is in the very expensive equipment needed to plant and harvest the tubers, and specialized structures in which to store them as they proceed over a stretch of months to market. The landowners who rent out to growers get to use their ground in the intervening years for other crops, including wheat, but especially those like alfalfa and legumes that help to put nitrogen back in the soil.

It's a system that works well, particularly for mid-level farmers who can't afford the cost of potato equipment and who plant those other irrigated crops between spud seasons. It also works for growers who can't afford the cost of the land but can get annual crops by checker-spotting their rentals to coordinate with fields where potato years are coming available.

If you're expert at this, and Frank is, you can make a good living. If not, you can literally go broke, and worse, as we'll see a bit later. The unstoppable infection of the Irish potato blight is a thing of the past, but the market can kill a crop's value almost as easily. Which is what happened to the popular growing of sugar beets when the U & I refinery in nearby Moses Lake shut down without adequate warning in 1978. Many growers lost their land in the fallout. But those who had stuck to potatoes survived, among them Mr. Martinez.

Frank's ancestry is in the Mexican state of Nuevo Leon, chiefly in five villages in Los Ramones County. By 1956, ten families from those villages were working as migrant field labor in the United States. Frank was five years old then, and already helping in the fields. And his family trekked north into Washington. In a typical year, they cultivated asparagus and thinned sugar beets around Sunnyside, halfway between Kennewick and Yakima, from March to June. Then it was out toward the coast, Mt. Vernon and Burlington, for strawberries through July. They picked green beans and berries around Salem, Oregon, from August to mid-September, then headed south to California's Fresno area for the raisins and wine grapes. By the end of October they'd be in Arizona for the cotton, and then back to Mexico. As they moved along, they had to live in housing just as cramped and decrepit as you can imagine. And because of the constant relocation, schooling was also a problem. Frank quit after the seventh grade.

As late as the 1950s, seasonal agricultural jobs a step up from field labor—operating harvest equipment and staffing canneries—were still mainly the province of itinerant Anglos who followed the ripening crops northward. Already, though, that supply of labor was shrinking. So also was the willingness of Mexican families to undertake such onerous round trips each year. Frank's parents decided to make the move permanent in 1966, choosing

Washington for their new home. "Down near the Texas border," Frank recalls, "the discrimination was bad. Here, not so bad."

And here his experience counted. By age seventeen, he was a field foreman for the potato processing corporation Skone & Conners. Thirteen years later, he was on his own, operating in the dicey middle of the spud business—contracting with land-owners for use of their ground to grow a potato crop, and with the processors for buying it. Now he harvests ten 125-acre circles a year, five in Adams County and five in next door Lincoln. He has two big "storages," as they're called, enormous long sheds looking a bit like slope-sided airplane hangars, which hold his annual production of up to 26,000 tons of potatoes. The Russet Burbank variety that he grows can be piled pretty high—up to eighteen feet—if it's done carefully: "You can't drop them more than a foot, to keep from bruising," says Frank. But when lay-ered neatly by loading machinery, they do rest comfortably atop each other. And with temperature control and ventilating fans at work, they can lie dormant for as long as six months as ship-ments deplete their stacks. (Why the bottom layers don't get mashed is one of nature's little mysteries. Potatoes turn out to be tough as well as ugly).

They're also much more diversified than you'd think. The list of varieties grown in Washington alone makes almost a tone poem:

Adora, Alaska Frostless, All Blue, All Red, Alturas, Atlantic, Avalanch, Banana, Banana Fingerling, Burbank, Butte, Cal Red, Cal White, Candy Cane, Caribe, Carola, Cascade, Cherry Red, Chieftain, Chieftain Elite II, Chieftain Elite III, Dark Red Norland, Désirée, Epicure, French Fingerling, German Butter-ball, Huckleberry, Ilona, Kennebec, Kern Toro, Kerrs Pink, La Ratte, Molli, Mondial, Nooksack, Nordonna, Norgold Russet,

Oscar, Pike, Pink Pearl, Provento, Purple Peruvian, Purple Viking, Ranger, Red Lasoda, Red Pontiac, Red Ruby, Red Thumb, Reddale, Red Gold, Regis Summit, Rose Finn Apple, Rose Gold, Russet Burbank, Russet Norkotah, Russet Norkotah 3, Russian Banana, Satina, Shepody, Sirius, Tejon, Tom Boy, Umatilla, Warba, White Rose, Yagana, Yellow Finn, Yukon Gold.[2]

The Russets that Frank favors are the variety of choice for the frozen products market—safe, reliable, good for storing and processing. Which fits well with his approach to the business. When last I saw him, at the farm where he stores his equipment (ten semi trucks, a number of tractors, three potato harvesters at $150,000 per monster machine), he was rewarding his year-round crew for faithful and successful work by preparing to transport all five of them and their spouses—along with him and his wife, Diana—to Las Vegas for a weekend extravaganza.

"Do you gamble there?" I asked.

"Me? Not really," he said. "There's too much of a gamble right here. The harvest . . . even in the storage, something can go wrong."

Or in the marketing, if, unlike Frank, the grower is not astute.

Some of Adams's potatoes go to the fresh market. But most are fed through relatively amazing machinery—steam peelers, water knives, photo-optic automatic defect removers—ending up as fries, tots, flakes, you name it. They're grown for a specific processor at a contracted price, which is the only protection available from market fluctuations: there are no federal subsidies and price protections for spuds, as there are for grain, corn, and other commodity crops.

But sometimes a farmer will go for "open potatoes"—growing without a contract in the hopes of getting a better price on the open market at harvest time or during storage. It's a bet that growers such as Frank Martinez won't make because the converse is getting a price lower than the cost of production—and paying the consequences. As noted in chapter 5, a losing gamble on open potatoes shifted big swaths of historically Phillips land into the hands of relative newcomers, the Ochoas, and the Hutterites. It was one of the most memorable transfers of Adams County's land ownership since the demise of the sugar beet factory. But in this case the change in ownership did not result in change of crop. The former Phillips acres are still, in rotation, producing potatoes.

That wrenching transfer has not been repeated on any major scale. Frank Martinez is not alone among established growers in knowing how to play the market well, but play it safe. And that's not easy. Even within the seeming comfort zone of contract growing there are dangers. Quality of the crop, says Frank, is one thing that winnows out unsuccessful growers. Bring in a substandard crop, and you won't get contracts the next year.

But there are factors also well beyond the influence of a grower's skill. Market concentration, for one. "There used to be a bunch of processors," says Roger Krug, who formerly was a buyer for one of the biggest, Lamb Weston. "And there was competition for the crop, and a grower could compare bids. But now it's down to just a few, and they rule the roost." These are corporations well listed in national corporate evaluations: Simplot, McCain's, Lamb Weston.

Frank Martinez confirms the impact of the tightening of demand sources. "We used to shoot for $500 an acre net on a crop, twenty-five years ago. Now it's down to $300. They always find a way to screw you."

Roger Krug confirms that. Roger, the Development Analyst for Adams County, grew up farming and worked for quite a while in the potato industry. As a buyer for Lamb Weston, he says, he did indeed hold a hard line for his company in dealing with growers. But he insists that the screwing was a two-level business, starting at the consumption end. Krug notes that the major burger chains who buy so much of Adams's output put a damper on demand simply by reducing the amount of fries in a standard serving. Reduced price to customers? Of course not! Depressed payment to processors, and hence to growers, yes indeed.

Amazing how something so small as fewer fried sticks in a cardboard holder can have such big impact, all the way back to an irrigated field in the Columbia Basin.

Roger's involvement with spuds began in the earliest days of irrigation, back when you siphoned water out of the canal for each row, known as the back-breaking method, and the Model T innovation that replaced it—wheeled lines of sprinkler pipe that rolled straight ahead down the field. He's a true font of information about the potato business and the people in it. He's also an irrepressible storyteller and joker. Six feet tall, now white-haired and balding, he played tackle on his college football team, and that physique is still there, albeit softened somewhat by his affection for burgers and, of course, fries. (He also has considerable affection for the Russian delicacies cooked by his wife, Svetlana.)

In his work for Lamb Weston, Roger would estimate the forthcoming crop by flying—he's a pilot himself—over the irrigated territory, counting the circles with potatoes in leaf. He also has grown them (and still has a small patch at his home in Pasco), has taught the culturing of the crop to college students, and, on both governmental and private-industry assignments, has advised growers and processors in the former Soviet Union—where he met and married Svetlana.

Roger also has a great interest in local people and events in Adams and neighboring counties. He's a walking encyclopedia of family and farm history, and particularly likes to recount bizarre episodes from times past—including those involving him. Such as how he discovered that the wheelbase of his father's '58 Chevy exactly fit the rails of an abandoned spur of the Union Pacific Railroad, on which he and teenaged friends then took daredevil rides. Or the dance back in the 1960s at the Sand Hills Grange where these ostensibly innocent bucolic youth got so plastered on sloe gin that they ended up butting their heads through the slatted seats of the folding chairs.

"So," I said, "during those days when the people back in San Francisco were wearing long hair and dropping acid and popping pills and stuff, you guys were out here popping chairs?"

"Popping chairs. It's kind of a rural mentality."

I doubt that many in the cohort of settler descendants would agree with that characterization of rurality, preferring to cite Roger's own mentality. And it's true that Roger does have considerable appreciation for the absurd, and does not shrink from indulging in it himself. I last saw him at the Fourth of July parade in Ritzville, in which the Chamber of Commerce contingent traditionally marches in clown outfits (don't ask). So there was realtor Audrey Schiable, in face paint and what could have passed for a hazmat suit from Wonder Bread, with giant multi-colored polka dots. And Roger, in ankle boots, bermuda shorts, a crazy-colored T-shirt, a bit of face paint, wearing a plastic wild boar's head for a crown—snout, tusks and all. As is the custom with all parade participants in this area, they carried bags of Halloween-type candy to throw to the streetside observers.

But in his regular working hours—which include many miles traveled daily along the local roads—Roger is charged with finding much more substantial benefits for the county: governmental projects, desperately needed light industry, something to stave off the economic decline plaguing everywhere but Othello.

And Othello's prosperity in that regard echoes the wheel of fortune's spin toward the modern motif of the top layer of American agriculture: *get big, or get out.* Here in the west end of Adams County, the packing plants and the immigrant factory work force await the potatoes and other crops made possible by irrigation, the costs of which have added new speed to the mechanization treadmill that has defeated so many small farmers nationwide.

That dynamic holds true also in Adams's more expansive drylands, of course, where so much more acreage is needed now to sustain a family than just fifty years ago. But here in the territory of crop circles, the effort to make a go of it with irrigation takes less land, yet just as much capital investment as for those dryland families.

And here also, we find another, very different, but equally, alternatively successful approach to winning a lifestyle from Adams's soil, dry or wet. It's the communal farming of the Hutterites, the Anabaptist Christian sect whose arrival in Adams County was roughly contemporaneous with that of the first Hispanic emigrants.

But the Hutterites, their intensely productive farming colonies birthing others in a steady, hop-scotching progress westward from eighteenth-century Europe, came in as buyers of existing farm acreage, supplying their own work force. And their unusual collective economics have lofted them to the top listing of landowners in Adams County.

10

The Fruitful Descendants of Ammann, Hutter, and Menno

Adams County took on a whole new personal dimension for me when I learned about the Hutterite colonies there—and settlements also of Mennonites, their Anabaptist religious cousins.

My mother was born to Mennonites, and even though she left that church while in college, she conveyed to me and my siblings the denomination's precepts of humanity, nonviolence, and responsibility. Part of my growing up—a part I fondly remember—was trips from our place in Maryland to her childhood home in Indiana (a wonderful train ride on the old Baltimore and Ohio line). Indiana, where milk was fresh from the cow and, in early summer, tasted badly of green onions. And where my grandmother still wore the light cap of netting that her largely emancipated sector of the Mennonite faith still required women to don during worship services as a minimal salute to church doctrine.

Of course, that cap was almost insignificant compared to the head coverings and other apparel requirements that have been imposed on women (men too, but less so) by every old-line religion from Christianity to Judaism, Islam, Hinduism, and Buddhism. But an outerwear bonnet also was in the church's favored wardrobe, and the concept of such requirements and the subordination they implied was too much for my mother—that, and some other aspects of sectarian doctrine—so she quit and became mostly secular. And that cleared the way for her to meet and marry my father, the unchurched son of a Scotch-Irish Presbyterian minister.

In the eighteenth century, my mother's ancestors lived in Germanic lands near today's French border, in what's now called the Rhineland Palatinate. There they were persecuted like all Anabaptists for their belief in biblical rather than ecclesiastical authority, and their insistence that baptism should be performed only when people are old enough to understand its significance and the commitment it requires. So in the 1700s, escaping, they came over to Pennsylvania. It was not a sanctuary. They were persecuted again for their refusal to forswear allegiance to their nominal protector, King George, during the American Revolution. They were caught in the doctrinal bind that has brought them torment for centuries. Anabaptists accept taxation and obedience to civil authority—a doctrine sometimes bespoken as "render unto Caesar what is Caesar's, render unto God what is God's"—but their firm acceptance of the biblical instruction "thou shalt not kill" requires them to refuse military service. So, unwilling to fight for either side in the conflict, many fled from the revolutionary strife to Canada, my mother's ancestors among them. In 1896, though, my great-grandmother returned to marry in a community of Mennonites who had stayed in what had become Indiana.

My father's forebears came from eternally troubled Ulster province in Ireland, where British kings had encouraged settlement by Protestant Scots to undercut the ruling Catholic nobility. My father's people, unhappy with the tensions of the place, emigrated also in the 1700s. They settled in southern Appalachia, which became a kind of second Scotch-Irish home-land. One claim to family fame was a distant relationship to Casey Jones, the locomotive engineer of folksong fame who barely saved his fireman before crashing fatally into a parked train. My grandfather, George, was a dynamic public speaker, a headliner for a while in the traveling Chatauqua tent shows of the early 1900s, my teenaged father sometimes accompanying him as a canvas wrangler.

But that brief ebullient era was the high-water mark for George H. Turner. Earlier, Grandpa had shepherded a dispersed flock in Pennsylvania, traveling rural byways in an old high-sided Ford. Grandma always drove—that's the way she was—even though she wasn't very good at it, and once on a narrow road in coal country she got the car flopped forty-five degrees over against the roadside cutbank. She managed to climb out—Grandpa and the kids, my father and his three sisters, were all tumbled up in the car—and ran off for assistance shouting "Help, help, there's a great big fat man stuck in there!"

That's the way she was, too.

And then for a while, Grandpa's ministry brought him and the family to Idaho, just a state line and two counties away from my beloved Adams County. My father remembered little of that residence, except for the time his parents drove off for a week-end revival leaving the kids at home with, among other things, a pot of freshly baked beans for food. Old-time ceramic bean pots came with a clamp to prevent them from boiling over while cooking, and my grandparents left it clamped shut. But we all know about cooked beans and gas and, yes, when the kids didn't open it in time, it duly exploded, blowing its contents all over the larder.

Bean eruptions aside, there was a good deal of loneliness at this ministerial posting. So Dad retained no fondness for that part of the West. But slight though it was, that bit of history, his family's time there, paired with my mother's Mennonite background as a kind of parental parenthesis around my own affection for dryland Adams.

The maternal connection came clearer when I visited the cemetery, all that's left of the former Adams County town of Menno. It was named for Menno Simons, an early Dutch inspirator of the denomination. There in a lonely, nearly treeless but well-tended site at a crossroads sit grave markers bearing the German names of families who share my ancestral religious origins, although many took a more circuitous route—through the Caucasus—to come here.

The town may be gone, but the church—the Menno Mennonite Church—actively continues. It combines what used to be three dispersed congregations, and it is quite a presence, miles from any other structure, sited amidst a windbreak and further array of trees atop a rise surrounded by rolling fields. The original church structure, built in 1908, was decommissioned and hauled to Lind for re-use. This substantial replacement—church, parish hall, and pastor's residence—bears the date of 1950. The architecture says that too, with its slanting green aluminum roofs, slotted windows, and cream-painted cement block walls. A flat grass lawn the size of a football field stretches beside the compound of buildings, and that is the site of the renowned annual Mennonite Country Auction. This event is the principal way in which the congregation raises money for domestic and international relief efforts of the Mennonite Central Committee, projects ranging from help for flood victims to support of indigenous schools and many other charitable causes.

The Country Auction is like a small fair without the carnival rides. Booths abound where you can buy some excellent pie and sausage and Germanic varieties of rural cooking. Eat and then bid for an assortment of the finest quilts and other handcrafts you can hope to see—the modern continuity of skills passed down through the generations of these farming people. It's handwork that expresses the makers' sense of the fine, the perfect, the beautiful as appropriate guides in producing even the necessities of everyday life. And it draws hundreds of eager bidders from all around the region.

This outpouring of individual and communal effort for the benefit of others gave me pride in my heritage, as did Pastor Terry Rediger's assurance that, despite the dominant Republican politics of this county and its neighbors, no one in his congregation had broken the Mennonite vows of pacifism to support the war on Iraq.

But the strongest poignancy of my Mennonite connection came clear at Menno's harvest celebration—a Sunday service followed by a dinner. I was welcomed at both and, with that welcome around me found myself opened to emotions near tears as the context brought strong memories. My mother had told me of one of her great aunts, I believe it was, in Canada, who died at an old age. And the Mennonite community there expressed its respect and love for the fruitfulness of her life by burying her with a bouquet of wheat.

And then there was the funeral in Indiana of my Uncle Harold Bender, a leading theologian, educator, and activist within the international Mennonite communion. Mourners came from so many places. I remember particularly farmers from Alberta, nearly a thousand miles away in Canada. They were in suits and ties. But there were also men and women in plain dress, guys with bowl haircuts and women in caps. And they sang, oh yes, they sang. Mennonites don't employ organs or other musical instruments, so the music in their services is a cappella singing, and it was harmonic and glorious.

Just as it had been, if from a smaller number of throats, at the Menno harvest service. And afterwards there, we sat at long tables for a copious supper—just as we had in Indiana after my uncle's funeral service. In Indiana, that supper had surrounded my uncle's open casket, in plain view with gauze draped from the lid to keep away flies. At first I had found that postmortem presence off-putting, but came to understand it as a kind of communion.

At Menno, even though I was merely an admirer—an outsider, a visitor, and did not share the doctrines nor even the basic Christian beliefs of the congregation—at the harvest dinner I could feel that sense of communion nonetheless with these friendly Adams County denizens, folks who construed their farming lives in the same religious context as had my mother's people for all these hundreds of years.

And it was my uncle Harold's name and reputation that eased the way for an interview with John Stahl, the farm Boss (there's also a Preacher, the religious leader) of the Stahl Hutterian Brethren. Such access is not a privilege that is readily granted. Gradually, though, Hutterites have found that some media exposure is to their benefit, lifting the self-imposed veil that tempts neighbors to see them as cultish, privileged in tax matters, and collectively antithetical to the norms of American society.

Well, they're not a cult. They're a communal religious denomination that impressively has stayed intact since the sixteenth century, breaking all records in Christendom outside of monastic orders for constancy of adherence to original beliefs and the social structure built therefrom. And in the case of the Hutterian Brotherhood, as they're formally known, that social structure rests on group common ownership of property and resources—an arrangement which they see as ordained by their revered Jesus.

Uninformed critics, sometimes neighbors, carp that that premise, stripped of its religious overlay, is really an insidious form of the dreaded communism. But it's really communalism, and the religious component is inseparable. As to political implications? By most knowledgeable assessments, in Adams County Hutterites tend to favor Republicans.

Stop me from asking how can this be (and would the Republicans who take their support endorse their choice of lifestyle?). Let's just say that the "Hoots," as they're known by some of their neighbors ("Hutterans" is another nom d'choice) are first of all excellent, innovative farmers, and along with that, very astute in the business end of agriculture. They are the living proof that —despite the failures of agnostic idealists' Brook Farm in the 1800s, and the demise in the the the U.S. Northeast of the wonderfully skillful and religious Shakers—communal agricultural societies not only can succeed, but can do right well. Moreover, Hutterites daily demonstrate that the seeming anachronisms of their religiously integrated lifestyle are no hindrance to a thoroughly modern approach to farming and its economics.

These are people who conduct their religious services in German, and the centerpiece of their worship is the reading of one or another of sermons written in the sixteenth century by early Hutterian leaders. Men and women sit separately in church, and for meals, which are communal. Women's dresses are long, and they wear headscarves. Those scarves can be polka-dotted , and the dresses can show floral print, but always against a dark background. Men also wear head coverings, sometimes billed caps but usually broad-brimmed hats—straw acceptable for workdays, but black felt always otherwise. Their shirts may have patterns any western gent might wear. But on days of worship, men's shirts are white, and outerwear for both sexes is black. Men are clean-shaven until they marry, and then grow beards (mustaches verboten). Hutterites live in extended structures of side-to-side single family apartments. Children, who learn both English and German, are schooled within the community all the way through twelfth grade, with teachers from "outside" hired to ensure that the state-mandated curriculum is taught along with religious instruction. That traditional component is provided by the colony's own teaching members.

But education for Hutterite children is not confined to church and schoolroom. From the earliest time that they're able, these kids observe, and then participate in the craft work, the gardening, handling of animals and food preparation, all the tasks that sustain the colony. And of course they learn the chores and skills of farming.

It's all very efficient and, to the colony members themselves, obviously satisfying—a reality that surprises outsiders who see the communal lifestyle's restrictions and separation from mainstream culture as repressive, even stifling. But the contrary evidence is overwhelming: the social and personal rewards of membership in this worshipful collectivity have carried the basic cultural design forward through four centuries.

Which highlights the most remarkable aspect of the Hutterites and their Anabaptist co-religionists: their continuity—the fact that despite persecution and vilification suffered for their beliefs right up into the 1900s, they have survived denominationally, with faith and social convictions intact. In their earliest times they were hunted and punished for daring to challenge established religious dogma and the institutional church. They were literally slaughtered for their resistance to clerical authority, their insistence on offering baptism only to consenting adults, and for hewing to biblical principles that emphasized human sharing and cooperation. For these "sins" alone, a Hutterite population estimated at twenty thousand in the early 1700s in Moravia (now part of Czechoslovakia) had been genocidally reduced to a mere nineteen survivors—the founders of the continuing branches of the Brotherhood.[1]

As the age of European nation states emerged, however, Anabaptists' doctrinal insults to dominant ecclesiastical authority became less important than their refusal to perform military service, or even to don uniforms. These practices were an extension of their fundamental opposition to taking human life. And for thus adhering to their pacifist principles, Anabaptists have been persecuted right up into mid-twentieth century, when the status of conscientious objector was finally accepted as a legitimate basis for refusing to take up arms. Chapter 9 related how the Russian Tsar's removal of this protection sent Anabaptists and other Russian Germans to America in the first place. I've mentioned that pressure to relent from this stance during the American Revolution drove my mother's forebears from Pennsylvania to Canada. But during the First World War, the German-speaking Hutterites became a particular target of jingoistic patriotism. That was when they began their most recent relocation from the United States to Canada, propelled by public outcry, vandalism, and some famous incidents of suffering. In one very ugly foretaste of 2004's indecencies in Iraq's Abu Ghuraib prison, three Hutterite brothers who refused to wear the army uniform or otherwise support the World War I effort were federally imprisoned and tortured—stripped to underwear, strung up by their hands at a height that let only their toes touch the floor, and denied all but minimal food until, still refusing to break their faith, they succumbed to malnutrition, pneumonia, and death.[2]

The same strain of tenacity has found its way into the Anabaptists' dedication to the integration of their religion with the demands of agriculture. All the major denominations have prospered in the New World (and there are numerous Mennonite settlements in South America as well as the United States), albeit via different strategies. Typically, the members of these churches, immersed in the sociocultural tenets of their faith, have proven very adept at winning livelihoods from the land. But only the Hutterites have done so in a way that successfully enables continued agricultural expansion within their credo.

The Amish, concentrated mainly in Pennsylvania (they're formally Old Order Amish Mennonites), are famous for their excellent farming and handcrafts and for their religiously-based refusal to use internal combustion engines, electricity, telephones, even buttons on their garments (vs. hook-and-eye closures). They continue to demonstrate that a family-sized farm can be sustained by horses or mules, cows for milk, chickens to eat, and all the animals' collective manures, given generous rainfall and good soil on which to plant. But what happens when the children grow and marry and need their own farms? Even when Amish farmers have prospered sufficiently to expand their holdings, the available land can only be divided so many times before the parcels are too small to support a new family. So alternative economies are needed within the structure of the faith. For the Amish, some of that need is supplied by their very dependence on archaic equipment, produced as though power tools did not exist: the renowned horse-drawn buggies, related blacksmithing, harness-making for the draft animals, and all manner of muscle-powered carpentry.

Even that farm support realm, though, does not offer enough opportunity to satisfy and hold the growing surplus of Amish youngsters. Many now have to "work off" in the mainstream community, where the seductions of non-Amish life are proving powerful. The Anabaptist doctrine that awards baptism only to consenting adults has a flip side sometimes interpreted as permission for older teenagers to experiment with the blandishments of popular culture before making their final acceptance of the faith. That process has always produced some straying from the religious fold. But the naturally-bred shortage of opportunities for productive work—farming or otherwise—within the Amish communities themselves has added difficulty to the choice of commitment to return.

For General Conference Mennonites such as the Menno congregation in Adams, the problem has similar economic roots, but starts from a different cultural plateau. Menno's congregants, who wear standard modern apparel, and whose children attend public schools, own individual farmsteads as the Amish do. Again, only if the parents have prospered sufficiently to acquire more acreage will there be enough land to support the children's separate families on the home ground. And then what of the next generation? In the case of Adams's Mennonites, their greater exposure to, and integration into popular culture enables their children much more easily to consider lives away from farming in the larger economy.

All of which has put Mennonites into the same bind as farmers of all other denominations who find that some of their children choose not to farm, but still inherit ownership in the home ground. Notably, far more than the much-maligned inheritance tax, which any astute farming family can avoid, this problem of allocating a fixed amount of land (or its value) amongst a growing number of inheritors has forced the sale of family-held farmground.

Thus it was, says Stahl Hutterian Brotherhood's farm Boss John Stahl, that much of the land that the colony acquired when branching south from Alberta in the 1980s was ground southwest of Lind sold by Mennonite widows who needed to cash out their acreage in order to distribute family shares.

Stahl himself was born in Montana, and had moved north to Canada with his parents as a youngster. But his birthright American citizenship made re-entry no problem. A stocky, plain-faced man with a fringe of white beard, he sat at a desk in the colony's utilitarian office as we talked. The telephone interrupted periodically, and he conversed with his callers in German. In between these calls, he unhesitatingly answered my questions about Hutterian life, and among other things explained why the problems of family continuity and inheritance that put Mennonite land up for sale do not afflict Hutterites. All value in a Hutterian colony's holdings is shared equally among its members. "If this place were to be sold tomorrow," said Stahl, "I wouldn't get any more than the smallest child."[3]

If experience is any guide, though, no Hutterite colony will ever be sold. Hutterites simply prosper. They don't use birth control, so their numbers do increase faster than the population at large. Consequently, colony memberships grow until the land they're farming, even if expanded, doesn't need all the available labor. "If there's not enough work for everybody," says John Stahl, "well, the devil is going to give them work. Idleness is the devil's playground."

That tip-over point usually comes when a colony's population reaches about 120. Then the home group uses accumulated fiscal resources, plus the endorsement of the regional diocese, to back its banking credentials, and acquires more land in a suitable place for a spin-off colony. The membership splits, and the existing colony gives aid and support to the contingent going away to start its new community on the freshly purchased ground.

Thus, since their 1870s arrival in Canada, Hutterites have moved in new-colony steps across that country to Alberta, down into Montana, and then westward into Washington and, now,

Oregon. And as they have moved through time across the map, they have taken advantage of the latest and most productive developments in agricultural technology. Not for them the Amish horse and buggy: only the best and most efficient of trucks, tractors, combines. They abjure television, but use cell phones and radio, global positioning equipment for their plowing, and the latest computer programming for managing their cropping and dairies. There's no on-line access for the members, however. "We don't go into the internet," says John Stahl. "There's too much junk on it. We don't want the kids to know that."

The Hutterites' use of technology also backstops their determined self-reliance. These communal people grow, harvest, and slaughter most of the food they eat, create their own clothing, and construct their communities' housing and work structures. So it was that at the Warden Hutterians' homeplace, ten miles north of the Stahl compound, I visited a state-of-the-art wood shop, a small factory really, which produces furniture for trade to other colonies. Those colonies reciprocate with their specialized production of other commonly used items, such as boots and shoes.

I visited Warden at the invitation of Barbara Gross, a widowed eldress who runs the colony's food services. She's also a kind of ambassador to the nearest city, Lind, bringing baked goods and her cheerful presence to community events. (The Hutterites are definitely aware of the need for positive interaction with their noncommunal neighbors.)

But at home, at the Warden Colony, Barbara supervises the women who plant and tend the big vegetable gardens, the men who slaughter the cattle, sheep and chickens, and the cooks and preparers who ready meals three times a day for ninety hungry people. No wood stoves or iceboxes here: stainless steel everywhere, a big walk-in freezer, restaurant-grade cooking ranges, and hose-equipped sinks. In the communal dining room, the blessing is said in German, but here in the kitchen, as in the wood shop, as in the mechanized field work, that ancestral continuity finds a comfortable mesh with modernity, the Hutterites doing the Lord's work in the most efficient way that the evolving world of technology makes possible.

Such progress, unfortunately, has brought them into trouble with one of their chosen modes of modern farming: crop circle irrigation. The trouble is water—a problem, oddly, that involves both surplus and shortage.

On the surplus side, the Stahl colony has a very innovative arrangement with potato processing companies in Othello that pipe waterborne production waste out to settling ponds on Hutterite land (and that of some neighboring farms). The ponds smell terrible as the potato detritus decomposes, but they're situated far away from human habitation. The sludge that settles makes good fertilizer, and the liberated water gets sprayed onto the colony's alfalfa fields, which feed the dairy cattle.

Sadly, though, both the sludge and the water are heavy with condensed natural salts that eventually will render useless the ground they're put on. At some point, this ostensible solution for both the colony and the processors will have to cease.

But that dilemma is minor compared to the larger challenge facing not only the Hutterites but adjacent noncommunal irrigating farmers as well. Both the Stahl and Warden colonies farm some dryland, but both substantially use pumped well water to irrigate many of their crops. And the underground aquifers that they and their circle-sprinkling neighbors are depending on are all too rapidly sinking away.

It's a cosmic irony, but in this land created by floods, the earth's available water supply is drying up.

11

Vanishing Lifeblood

It has become clear that the groundwater, the subsurface aquifer system underlying Adams and surrounding counties, is being depleted.[1] But opinions among water users as to the seriousness of the problem, its causes, and ways to confront it, well . . . it's a bit like the fable about blindfolded men trying to identify an elephant by touching its parts. The man pressing on a leg declares the unknown object to be a tree. The guy holding the trunk says it's a hose. And he who palpates a tusk asserts that the creature is a spear.

In the case of the diminishing water supply, there are no blindfolds. But people do experience the situation in markedly different ways depending on what crops they grow, and precisely where they live. Even among those who agree that there's a problem, there's disagreement about how to deal with it, and the likely outcome if they don't.

And there are some who simply deny it. One state government official, for instance, told me that the Columbia Basin's underground aquifers are recharged by annual rainfall. Not true. And in the category of wishful thinking, the manager of one of the largest of Adams's irrigated farming operations asserted that there's no danger because enough new water comes in with runoff from the mountains north of Spokane. Also not true.

There's legitimate basis for some confusion, however, in that there are some farmers who don't experience direct impact from the problem. The home well at the Plagers', for instance, down in the Paha Coulee (see chapter 3), is still putting out the fifty gallons a minute it did in 1927. And Mike Miller, who crops three sprinkled circles some miles northwest of Ritzville (plus dryland acreage and cattle), finds useable water just eighty feet down for his home well, and points out a location near one of his fields where, in a draw, there's actual surface-level seepage in springtime if you dig a hole. "We're right on the edge of an aquifer [channel]," says Mike. The surface seepage and high-water table here don't help with irrigation, which takes vastly more gallons than any seep could provide. But it does demonstrate that folds, bends, and pockets in the subsurface strata can bring the precious fluid closer to topside in some places than others. Thus Mike's crop circle pumps have a much easier task than those of neighbors only miles away. "Our wells are just 250 feet and 400 feet down," says Mike. "We're a rare case of where it doesn't cost us an arm and a leg to get that water up."

"Rare" is the key word here. Other examples are more indicative of what's going on. Ten miles south of Mike Miller's place, at the bottom of the Bauer Coulee, what used to be a persistent small stream has dried up. And at the home farm of Mike's cousin Grant, south and east of Mike's place by twenty miles, the family's residential well recently had to be punched another one hundred feet down.

Those, however, are among the smaller indicators of the larger problem—that nature's own supply of water here isn't enough to sustain all the uses it's put to. Most prominently, in the west ends of Adams and neighboring counties north and south, irrigation wells are going dry either because they're costing too many arms and legs to drill deeper, or pump, or because they are, literally, hitting bottom—not running out of water, just running out of water that's useable.

Paul Stoker, Executive Director at the Columbia Basin Groundwater Management Area (GWMA) tells the story of a farmer up near Odessa, in neighboring Lincoln County, who drilled a well 2,200 feet deep, only to get very acidic water "that smells like rotten eggs, and he wishes he'd never spent half a million dollars to drill it." Besides its acidity, water from wells that deep has another serious detriment—it can come up as hot as 174 degrees (for comparison, the average home water heater runs no higher than 140 degrees).

Pass Paul Stoker on the street, and you might think he's on his way to a casting call for Mr. Average Guy—medium height, brown hair, pleasant, regular features. But he turns out to be an agricultural version of the Renaissance man: a former local farmer (sugar beets, among other crops) with a college background in accounting who has become expert in the disciplines of conservation. He officiates in state- and national-level organizations in that field. In person he's both knowledgeable and authoritative.

We meet in the GWMA conference room, its walls covered with detailed maps of irrigation zones. The chairs are padded, and comfortably recline (after a tentative test to make sure there's no backflip potential). As I cue my tape recorder, Paul tells me with a bit of asperity that because he does not have scientific academic credentials, I can only cite what he tells me about the aquifer's recharge problems as concepts, rather than facts. Then, cutting through the opinions and inaccuracies I've heard up to now, he gives me, at last, a useful picture of the hydrogeology that finally makes coherent sense out of all the different water-user experiences. And lo, he depicts a breakfast. The groundwater underlying Adams and surrounding counties lies in the Columbia Plateau Aquifer System, says Stoker, "and the best way to describe that is as a stack of pancakes."

Pancakes in a bowl, as it happens. Big bowl: the Columbia Basin, spanning a diameter of roughly 160 miles, with Adams County a bit off center in the lower left quadrant. It's a filled-in depression, sloping southwest from the Bitterroot Mountains of western Idaho, bordered around the compass, as previously noted, by the foothills of the Cascades to the west, the Selkirk Mountains above Spokane and the Blue Hills of northern Oregon. The surface of the geology that fills this Basin is the Columbia Plateau, the wide, dense spread of Noah's Gift, the wind-delivered silts from the Missoula floods. And piled below that deep surface deposit of soils lie the metaphorical pancakes. Massive pancakes: layers of basalt rock. Some one hundred have been mapped, of varying sizes and spreads, but the main structure of this underground formation is twenty-three vast slabs up to one hundred feet thick. Whether major or minor, the rock pancakes are separated by interbeds of gravel and dirt, at a ratio of about ten to one: one hundred feet of basalt, for instance, sits on maybe ten feet of interbed.

The groundwater is in those interbeds. How it got there is a long story. How, and to what extent it is replenished, is not fully known. And how long it will be there is an open question, because more is being pumped out every year than the sources of refill are putting back in. Crucially, how the agricultural communities of the Plateau deal with this problem will largely shape what the future holds for Adams County. (A recent estimate of the impact of a water shortage in the irrigated areas of Adams and Lincoln counties projected loss of 32 percent of the two counties' jobs, and annual economic loss of some $302 million.

The measurement in human terms would be just as dramatically severe.)[2]

You'd think that a history of gigantic floods would be enough in the category of natural wonders for any one geographical region. But no, the Columbia Basin has yet another claim to geological fame: vast, formative flows of lava, floods of molten rock as significant in their own way as the mighty aqueous inundations that carved the coulees and delivered the farmland. Even more prehistoric than the ancient floods, these eruptions—occurring millions of years ago—also lacked the cachet of, say, the funneled-up blast of Vesuvius, which destroyed Pompeii and Heraculaneum in 79 BC, or Indonesia's Krakatoa in 1883, which changed a whole year's weather for the entire Northern Hemisphere.

But the lack of the single-source explosion and pyroclastic flows of traditional cone-shaped volcanoes was more than offset by the sheer scope of what happened. The shifting of North America's subdural plates opened big fissures deep toward the earth's core in what is now the fringe of western Idaho. Major earthquakes accompanied the opening of these cracks, and when the splits occurred, molten magma sprayed and sheeted up to fall and flow thickly, red hot, across the terrain sloping west. There was more than enough of the erupting lava to go around. One estimate cited a cleft in the present Lewiston area a quarter-mile wide, forty miles long, that blew liquefied rock ten thousand feet in the air, expelling some 200,000 cubic miles of the stuff in sixty days.

It was not a good time for living creatures, animal or vegetable, on what was becoming the Columbia Plateau.

During the centuries, sometimes millennia, that followed these periodic eruptions, wind, water and vegetation worked to build layers of soil and gravel atop the hardened lava flows.

Geologists call this buildup *overburden*, rising above the hardened lava. Deservedly or not, the term gives stronger significance to whatever lies underneath—a concept that makes more sense in places like West Virginia, where, in strip mining, overburden is what you scoop away to get at seams of coal. Here, the overburden is, if anything, more significant than the basalt thickness it lies atop, because it is home to the water of the aquifer system. Rainfall and stream flow infused these accumulations, because in ancient eras the climate on the Plateau was both warmer and wetter than today, almost subtropical at times.

So the creative pattern repeated, again and again, over immense stretches of time. Eruption, cooling, gradual erosion; accumulation of gravels and soils, gradually infused over hundreds or thousands of years with water from rainfall and streamflow. And then—boom! On comes the next eruption, the next overwhelm of lava, entrapping the water in the newly created interbed, and severely altering and limiting the ways in which additional fluid can enter that former surface layer. Except at edges of the Basin, where sometimes interbeds were left exposed as the lava surged away downslope, there was no way for precipitation to soak through the new deposit of basalt rock.

But it was not a totally closed system. As Mike Miller's experience demonstrates, the lava that layered up over the interbeds was far from perfect in its coverage of the saturated material. There were fractures, buckled twists, thin spots, potholes that left fissures for upward seepage, but more importantly, openings for aqueous resupply to soak down and enter. The vast Missoula floods themselves, gouging out the coulees, put water into the interbeds they exposed. And the persistent erosive flow of rivers—the Columbia, Snake, Palouse, Walla Walla, Wenatchee, and their tributaries—infused the interbeds they cut through.

Envisioning the Basin's underground movements of water,

therefore, can seem inordinately complex. But that's only so if you want to understand every nook and cranny, as it were, every diversion from the general pattern. For purposes of everyday comprehension, Paul Stoker's explanation, via pancakes, still gives the best view. Pancakes drooped into a tipped bowl. Pancakes with the syrup surging toward the lowest levels of slope in the tilted pile.

The Columbia Plateau's southwesterly declination drops three-thousand feet from its highest edge in Idaho to the low point at Pasco, at the junction of the Snake and Columbia rivers. That creates an underground hydraulic gradient that increases urgency of flow as water in the interbeds obeys the demands of gravity and moves downhill, toward the lowest repository levels of the ancient lava deposits. And as that downward flow continues, as it has for centuries, it creates an artesian pressure— water pushed from behind to find the level at which it came into the aquifer.

Thus the ancient creation of the multilayered Columbia Plateau Aquifer System, with artesian pressure increasing the farther southwest you go. In Adams, that means highest pressure in the western third of the county, and particularly the Othello panhandle. So when the pumped irrigation trend developed there, farmers found copious supplies of upwardly inclined water at relatively reasonable depths.[3]

Increasingly, that is no longer the case.

Traveling across Adams's landscape from border to border, you're not often aware of the overall southwesterly slant—you mainly observe the rolling, up-and-down topography of loess mounds, the deep declivities of the coulees, and so forth. But you do notice when you've passed from the scab ground of cattle country into the county's middle third of dry wheatlands. And again, moving westward, you know when you've hit waterland—irrigation country, where fields suddenly begin to sport the big center pivot rigs. In season, when they're putting water on the ground, the display is worthy of some young engineer's artistic fantasy. The huge, gawky equipment looks like something made out of giant erector sets, but as the water mists up and out into sunlight, rainbow refractions form to amplify the simple aesthetic pleasure that airborne water gives anywhere, from splashes in stony mountain streams to fountains the world around—particularly here, where the display is so very much out of context in the arid landscape.

In fact, these big spraying machines are out of historical context too, a technological afterthought as regards the original irrigation plans for the Plateau. That scheme, timeless in concept, envisioned only a network of gravity flow canals, to be fed by damming the Columbia River out west of Spokane. Water would be sucked from the canals for "rill" irrigation, running down the rows of plowed fields.

Thus the Columbia Basin Project, a key public works component of Franklin D. Roosevelt's New Deal recovery effort to combat the thirties' Great Depression. The centerpiece was the enormous Grand Coulee Dam, constructed between 1934 and 1942. This huge monolith, for decades the largest concrete structure in the world ("The biggest damn thing ever built by a man," as Woody Guthrie put it in his ballad "Roll On, Columbia"). It was a multipurpose creation, designed for flood control and power generation as well as irrigation, and succeeded notably in all three categories. (It also put a permanent stop to the upstream run of the river's migrating salmon).

The dam ponded the river behind it into vast Lake Roosevelt, stretching 151 miles back to the Canadian border. But that water doesn't go directly to the fields. Instead, huge pumps move some of it up and over a rise into the dam's eponymous Grand

Coulee itself, where another dam twenty-seven miles farther along this huge channel creates the irrigation reservoir called Banks Lake. The two primary canals that service the westernmost Basin farms take off from this supplementary body of water. And in the fullest version of the irrigation plan, at least one other canal was supposed to bring water to the middle of Adams, as far as the Lind area.

That supply source was never built. To this day, though, there are hopeful advocates for its eventual construction. Glenn Stockwell, candidate for Adams County supervisor in 2006, campaigned principally on the call for a new canal. "I was always a Roosevelt Democrat," he told me, "but there's no chance of winning like that here. So I'm running as a Republican." He did not win the seat, but he was not alone in his concern with the issue.

The lack of the mid-county waterway became a rather moot point for a while as the technology for pumping and spraying evolved and spread. But, as Paul Stoker explains, that technology is the principal culprit in bringing the aquifer into peril.

I had thought that the biggest extractors from underground supplies were the processing plants, the freezers and the canneries where all the future edibles are heavily washed, the potatoes get cut up by water knives, cans of peas and so forth are filled with water, and the scrap and sludge of the processing is sluiced away. Surely those swilled the most, they and the towns, like Othello with its expansion plans including a golf course, a form of development renowned for great guzzling.

But no. "Most of the time," says Paul Stoker, "most of the time a city's or an industry's water uses are miniscule compared to what's used by [an irrigated] field. A city the size of Othello doesn't take any more water for all the different users it supplies than three or four crop circles, equal to whatever would have been irrigated if [the city's land] had a field on it. And the biggest processing plants I know, like McCain's and Carnation and those guys, gosh, they have one well. That's it. These guys can't use more than a field's worth of water, because what do you do with the water after you use it? That becomes your big problem. It's like Lamb Weston in Connell, they've got four, five circles out west of their building, where they have to spray the stuff out into the hay fields to get rid of it [like the Stahl Hutterites' arrangement, mentioned in chapter 10]. So you know how much water they use, because you can see what they do with it. You just can't use that much water in [the food preparation] process."

But the crop fields? "You should do the usage numbers in your book, because they're really mind-boggling to people. The average efficient irrigated field that raises potatoes under sprinklers here uses three acre-feet per year, per season, per acre. At an average of 125 acres per field, that's 160 million gallons goes on one field every year." Enough, in urban areas, for almost two thousand households. "Collectively, agricultural irrigation is removing half-a-million acre-feet of water out of the aquifer system every year." There obviously is some recharge, says Stoker (although most likely not in the deepest, most ancient interbeds), because otherwise the aquifer would be going down more quickly than it is. "But it's well documented that there's more water withdrawn than is being recharged. Our top layers are drying out."

Drying out, though, in the world of wells here, can refer to bank accounts as much as to the actual availability of water. Aside from the grotesque possibility of hitting unusably hot, smelly stuff if you go too far below, there's the simple fact that even aiming for deep interbeds above the useless zone involves enormous combined expense for additional drilling, more powerful pumps, and higher electricity bills—costs that can make it impractical to seek that supply. So some farmers shut down their failing wells and, if they're within range of enough rainfall, go back to dryland cropping. Or they can sell the water rights that attach to their land—the right, approved by the State, that is, to pump a certain amount annually from underground. In early days, these rights were automatic, unquestioned. No one measured the extraction. Since exhaustion of the aquifer has become noticeable, however, regulation has set in. Basically, no new wells are being approved. So, the right to pump groundwater—a right that can be sold separately from the land on which it was granted, and applied anywhere above the Basin's aquifer system—has become a prized item for sale.

And that can produce some unusual outcomes.

"Out here east of Rte. 395," says Stoker, "the water rights on a section of ground were sold by auction this spring They had a well there with a 1,300-gallon-a-minute permit, and it was only 500 feet deep, but it went dry. But they had a legal paper with a water right for those 1,300 gallons a minute. So rather than drill the well deeper, they turned the property into dryland and sold off the water right [for someone else to use for a well somewhere else]. That sort of defies logic, that you sold the rights to a dry well. But they did. For a quarter-million dollars."

In its own way, of course, that's no more illogical than the increasingly popular concept of selling air pollution credits, the arrangement by which a polluting source that brings its output below restricted levels can then sell the unused margin to a violator for profit—easing that violator's legal problems even as it continues to pour out pollutants. It's all in the New Age matrix of how the air we breathe and the water that makes up some 98 percent of our bodies, and is crucial to life at all levels, have become commodities. And the governing factor applying most obviously to water in this world of markets, is scarcity. Water is, after all, a finite resource. There's a lot of it, but so much of it is salty. Only three percent of the planet's water is fresh, with just under one-third of that amount in the ground. As farming on the Columbia Plateau illustrates, access to that fresh water can be difficult indeed, even where soils have been wonderfully prepared for its use in agriculture by, ironically, immense prehistoric flows of fresh water.

There are difficulties that the agronomists themselves produce in the equation. The nitrogen-based fertilizers and other chemicals that farmers plow into the soil do indeed work their way down to groundwater in some places, particularly into that layer of water lying atop the final spread of lava. That happens where those upper interbeds are easily reached, or by deeper interbed transfer resulting from tendencies of the water users themselves: haphazard drilling practices have made the underground "like swiss cheese," says Stoker. "There's twenty thousand wells drilled here in the last basically one hundred years in our four-county area. Twenty thousand wells too often to the lowest bidding well driller, which means that the lowest bidder didn't case the wells, because it costs money to case the wells. So as you go down through these pancakes, each one [with an open hole drilled through it] has access to the whole of the interbeds. So, if you think about hydraulic gradient, in many of the wells, the bigger ones especially, the water from, say you go down through five interbeds? Then the top four are draining into the bottom one twenty-four hours a day. Or it could be the other way. It depends on the gradient of that particular layer. But effectively, the water is draining out of some and going back into others, which is called 'cascading' inside of a well. And we have horrible problems here because of cascading. A lot of the reason for the top layers drying out is that our wells are basically draining each other. That's why many of the shallower domestic wells east of us have gone dry [or feeble, like Grant Miller's home well]. The people who have a house only needed five gallons a minute, went down only two hundred, three hundred feet for the water, then after a few years the well goes dry."

Cascading also can carry residue from fertilizers and herbicides into the upper levels of the aquifer, one source of the pollution problem largely responsible for the creation of GWMA. Much of the most easily accessible groundwater in the lower stretches of the Basin is showing worrisomely high levels of nitrates—the principal ingredient of fertilizers. This salty infusion comes almost entirely from irrigated crops. On dryland fields, there would need to be a highly unusual amount of precipitation to soak fertilizer down past the roots of the crop and on through the overburden. Only in shallow soil beds can this occasional natural saturation reach even the top layer of water-bearing soils—although surface runoff from snowmelt, particularly, can carry chemicals from dryland fields to streams that eventually do contribute to underground recharge.

But irrigation, of course, is equivalent to an unusual, even very unusual amount of rainfall. And the underground situation it creates is abnormal as regards aftereffects as well as the plenitude of encouragement it provides for a bountiful harvest. The denser the crop, the more fertilizer is needed to generate maximum yield. The more chemicals that are applied, the more that can leach down with this abundance of artificial precipitation.

The impact becomes particularly clear in the territory around Othello, where a bed of impervious clay spreads underground above the top layer of aquifer, preventing the irrigation soak from directly reaching groundwater. The clay is beneficial in that regard, perhaps, preventing direct downward leaching of chemicals. But it's problematic also because the water blocked from descending instead pools on top of the clay and tends to create a swamp. So, says Paul Stoker, farmers on thousands of irrigated fields have had to install drain tiles nine feet underground to lead the surplus fluid away. Where does it go? Some into the coulees, some into Scootenay and Potholes reservoirs, where dams increase the storage capacity of depressions chewed out by the ancient floods, and some to Rodeo Lake, west of Othello, which offers a rebuke of sorts to the whole business of putting water where nature refused it.

"Rodeo Lake, that's a water hazard," says Stoker. "See, all the irrigation out to the east of us saturates the soil on top, and it can't get through the blue clay, so it runs horizontally to the west, towards the Potholes. And some basalt layers surface just on the other side of Rodeo Lake, and that forces an end to the water movement, so it just pops up right there. It's water standing on top of the ground, and they can't even pump it fast enough to get rid of it." Moreover, in one of the many ironic twists in this unusual world of aquatics, Rodeo's buildup from irrigation is no help to the people next door, who could use it. Othello's city wells get their water from twelve hundred feet deep, says Stoker, and the levels from which they draw have dropped two hundred feet. But the unwanted surplus of Rodeo Lake never gets down there to help out.

Even if it did, this effluent drained down through the crop fields from the canals and sprinklers is too saturated with the residue of agriculture's chemistry to be useable for drinking and bathing, watering of livestock, or sustenance of wildlife.

That concern—the matter of pollution, fear of further pollution of the aquifer—was the main reason that GWMA was formed in 1997. But Stoker sees a misperception that the application of chemicals itself is the problem. He feels that the amounts of fertilizer and herbicides that farmers apply are well enough regulated—if only by the cost factor: the stuff is very expensive, so only a stupid grower would use more chemicals than a crop requires.

No, the main issue, he says, is the amount of irrigation that's applied. "Even if you use small amounts of chemicals and fertilizers, less than you should, if you use excess water you'll dissolve those soluble ions and take them south, down into the groundwater. That's why our main project here is to try to get irrigators to reduce their leachage, or the amount of water they pass through the root zone, to below five percent. And if you get that done, below five percent, you'll effectively not put enough volume of material to make any difference to the aquifer."

So, accepting Stoker's analysis, the pollution factor is manageable. But what about the other problem that has emerged as GWMA launched its studies—the shrinking availability of useable underground water to begin with, polluted or otherwise? The prognosis on that is not good, if current practices continue unchanged—most notably with Othello, Ritzville, and other municipalities vying for incoming industry, New Age processors of ethanol and biodiesel in particular.

"My opinion," says Stoker, "is that the critical element is to take those agricultural withdrawals off line on the aquifer system to allow there to be enough water available for such future activities. Because right now, the aquifer system is deteriorating."

But Stoker isn't advocating an end to irrigated agriculture in Adams County or the Basin in general—he's just calling for a new source of the fluid the crops crave. Not for him, though, the faded dream of more canals. Instead, a vision of pipelines, a network of conduits drawing from that promised Grand Coulee source. As he points out, pumping to sprinklers from such a relatively horizontal system will be vastly cheaper than sucking the water up from thousands of feet down. It's a long-term proposition, and expensive, but without it, there's trouble.

I asked Paul whether there's a predictable future point when it won't make sense any more to seek additional irrigation water supply from deep down below.

"We're at that point now," he said.

Epilogue

When I was a kid, movies used to be shown along with short subjects—cartoons, newsreels, and often enough, a travelogue. And those always seemed to end with the narrator intoning, "And so, as the sun sets behind the sheltering mountain, or across the beautiful bay, or casting its golden glow on the great cathedral, we leave with fond memories of this wonderful place." It was as though whatever locale we'd seen was frozen in time, just awaiting our visit.

Well, Adams County is a pretty neat place, but as we leave it, change, as ever, proceeds. There's always the slow blowing away of the land, of course, but on the more dynamic side of things, global forces are intruding—both the human sort, in the form of markets and trade, and the limits of the globe itself in the realm both of atmospheric warming and, more immediately, diminution of natural resources.

The Columbia Basin has joined a growing list of American agricultural regions where underground water is being mined—withdrawn faster than it's replaced. The problem has become severe in California's unparalleled multicrop Central Valley, where extraction from aquifers has dropped land surface levels by as much as twenty feet. And in that state's coastal swales of the Salinas and Pajaro rivers, carpeted with a richness of lettuce, strawberries, and artichokes, overpumping has begun sucking in seawater that pollutes the fresh underground flow.

Less publicized, but of much greater scope, is the draining down of the vast multistate midwestern Ogallala aquifer.

Nor is this just a homegrown problem. India, China, North Africa, and the Middle East all are afflicted by overstrain on their groundwater resources, not just in farming areas but in cities as well. Add to that the shortage of potable water in much of the developing world and you have the outline of a looming global crisis: thirst for what can be drunk, and what can be given to crops.

Nominally, Earth has plenty of water: it covers three-quarters of the globe's surface. But 97 percent of that is in the salty oceans. Of the three percent that's not salty, just over two-thirds is frozen in icecaps and glaciers. The greatest amount of what's left is in the ground. Rivers, lakes, and swamps hold less than one percent of the fresh water supply.

Above and beyond the question of water's types and where they're located is the mystery of why we have any at all. It surprises me that creationists, those who insist that earthly existence as we know it can only be explained by "intelligent design," have not chosen water as supportive evidence for their contention. The stuff is vital to all forms of the globe's plants and creatures. But science cannot say from whence it came.[1] Earth's normal planetary chemistry does not yield the amalgamation of H_2O—two hydrogen atoms and one of oxygen. If it did, we'd see new water being generated all the time. And that doesn't happen.[2] Fortunately, water is elemental in another way. Like energy, it's essentially indestructible We can play with it, creating heavy water (substituting deuterium for hydrogen), and we can pollute it beyond measure. We can move it from place to place, from mode to mode. Freeze it, you get ice. Boil it, you get steam. Melt the ice, condense the steam, you get water. We learned about the water cycle in elementary school: evaporation up, precipitation down. Pretty nearly the only way to get rid of the stuff is to seal it up as in airtight burial caskets (humans, after all, contain up to forty-two quarts of water, 60 to 70 percent of body weight). Out in the wild world, dying plants and animals return their bodily content to the soil. Arguably, some water vapor from the upper atmosphere may escape into space, lost to us. Otherwise, we're in a closed system. Down here below, we are simply recirculating what we have. There's a lot of it, but we aren't getting any more.

So how we handle what we have becomes the issue. It's when we alter the balance of that closed system that we run into trouble. Overdraw the groundwater supply, or pollute our fresh sources, and we have to find alternatives. Which is when finance begins to define necessity. "You know," says Paul Stoker, "it's all a matter of money. Whether you take the water that comes out of your toilet and clean it up good enough to reuse it, or you take the water out of the ocean and desalinize it to use, it's all a matter of money. Because water's water. You pour dirt in it, and then you clean the dirt out to re-use it, or use it as it is. And that's what happens here at these [potato processing] plants in Othello. They use it to wash things off, clean things up, and the water gets dirty. So it's cheaper right now to pump the dirty water out to a field than it is to clean it up. At what time in the future do we get to the point where it's cheaper to build a cleaning plant, and just re-use the water, instead of buying water? That's going to be an interesting transition. As water gets more and more valuable, eventually it'll get to the point that the input water costs more than cleaning up the water you've already got."

Increasingly in wealthy coastal places such as Saudi Arabia

and yes, California, the money choice is turning toward desalinization of seawater to supply growing thirst. Inland agricultural areas, though, don't have that option. And in those places, world around, when groundwater runs scarce, the pressure builds to capture surface flow behind dams. There's often the added justification of hydroelectric power production, and sometimes, as with Grand Coulee, flood control too. But consequences can be brutal for the local societies inundated in the process, and for the riverine ecologies destroyed by interrupting streamflow.

In the Columbia Basin, the "solution" of dams was selected before any groundwater problem was even known. Before any questions of ecological preservation were imagined, before impact on the Columbia's salmon fishery, crucial to riverside native populations, would even be considered as important. Contrary to what my farm owner boss Bob Phillips asserted, Grand Coulee water *was* meant to flow all the way to Lind in Adams County. It was, of course, a costly intent, and the reclamation planners and federal budgeters doubtless sighed with relief when pumped circle irrigation came to the fore, and seemed to make full development of the Columbia Basin Project unnecessary. But, as Paul Stoker points out, that alternative is running dry. So 2007 found the United States Bureau of Reclamation deep into a study of the various ways in which the original goal of more widespread distribution of Lake Roosevelt water can be accomplished.

Never too late, I guess, to complete a project begun almost seventy-five years earlier—a task both easier and more difficult now. Easier, because advances in technology do allow water delivery via pipes and pumps versus the carefully graded excavation of canals. Harder because environmental protections for the salmon runs and riverine ecology, and the demands for hydroelectric power production by Grand Coulee and the Columbia's downstream dams, have evolved to require precise levels of river flow that must be maintained regardless of seasonal fluctuations in upstream precipitation.

But the experts say that by trapping the river's winter surplus in new reservoirs, there will be enough summer volume to replace the amount being overdrafted from the aquifer. It's a snail's-pace race against time, though. The study of alternative modes and routes of delivery, the process of choosing the most efficient among those, assessing and mitigating environmental impact, and so forth, won't be completed until at least 2010. And the earliest thereafter that the water might begin to arrive? Probably 2015.

Meanwhile, the changing world is bringing new demands for the aquifer to satisfy biofuels production that has targeted the Basin. Roger Krug, Adams County's ever ebullient Development Analyst, runs down the list of probabilities: biodiesel refineries planned in Warden and Odessa, an ethanol plant in Tokio (just north of Ritzville), and others of both varieties in nearby counties to the west. I thought how good, how appropriate to turn wheat into alcohol. (Among other things, it makes a very good beer that carries the German name for its genesis: Hefeweizen.) But Roger quickly derailed my assumption that these new arrivals would make massive use of local crops for production. Barley, a comparatively minor component of the Basin's agrifamily, is an ethanol candidate, and more of it likely will be grown. But wheat isn't in the picture—it can indeed be refined into ethanol, but has a much smaller content of fermentable sugars than the most preferred ingredient, corn. And there is no local surplus of corn—a fair amount is grown in Washington, although not so much in the Basin, but it principally supplies the market for cattle and poultry feed.

As for biodiesel, that product comes from oilseeds, preferably canola or soy. And none of these are dryland crops (although experimentation is underway to develop a dry-farmed canola), and the local climate is not favorable to soy. So, incredibly, the supportive input for the Basin's new fuel plants will be mostly corn and soybeans shipped in by rail from the Midwest, and canola from Canada.

So why have these enterprises targeted Adams County and the Basin? The answer combines the incentive of state and federal development grants, and relatively inexpensive, available land, plus rail, barge, and highway proximity to northwest coastal markets. Eager available labor is another part of the equation. These plants will bring new jobs, more need for trucking, etc., and surely fuel corn will join the rotation schedules on irrigated ground (eventually, too, ethanol technology may evolve to make better use of non-irrigated crops. Switchgrass, for instance, another possible source of ethanol, currently classifies as a weed here. But it may well become a vintage for fuel.)

Even with the looming prospect of groundwater shortage until the new Basin Project supplies wash in, it seems certain that potatoes will continue to rule the crop list on the artificial wetlands. Dale Lathim, Executive Director of the Potato Growers of Washington, asserts that as existing wells go dry or become useless, demand for french fries and other processed products will displace other crops in circles that now don't grow the spuds—circles watered by the existing canals.

Some of that displacement may cut into the existing irrigated alfalfa crop, which would add to the financial burden that ethanol's demand for corn is imposing on the feed budget for ranchers like Jake Harder, and even more so the feedlots where they send their cattle to fatten.

And crop change is coming also to the dryland farms, even before any botanical breakthroughs yield parch-adapted oil seeds or alcohol-oriented biomass hybrids. Grain production and grain marketing globally has radically evolved. There are far more suppliers overseas than there used to be. China and Australia particularly have begun to export the very same soft white wheat that has been an Adams County specialty for decades.

At the same time, long-standing pressures from the World Trade Organization (WTO) for the United States to reduce its subsidization of commodity farm crops—so as to enable export competition from overseas producers—have put those supports in question.

Gretchen Borck, the Washington Wheat Growers' Issues Director, and a grower herself, shook her head resignedly. She sees a fairly bleak future trend that will cause further consolidation of land ownership, and continue the erosion of many towns—because, fundamentally, the outside world doesn't care. Congressional farm support legislation is up for renewal, and revision, and she foresees reduction of price supports in accordance with WTO demands. "Farmers are only one percent of the U.S. population now," she said. "We feed the rest, but [politically] we don't matter. I tell my growers you're not going to have your commodity payments. They don't want to hear that. But the [new] farm bill is going to be very green."

She means that future farm legislation will shift more toward preservation of the land, taking acreage out of production as the United States begins to depend more and more on imported food. What would that mean for Adams and surrounding dryland farm country? Likely, indeed, more fields going into the federal conservation reserve programs, among other reasons because the average age of Washington's wheat farmers reached fifty-nine in 2005. Within a decade much of the land will be passing on to new ownership that may not be local. Not every retiring farmer has children who want to continue growing crops. And when farm owners die, children who share the inheritance may compel a liquidation even if one of them wants to keep on (although seemingly there's as great or greater likelihood that the siblings who continue cropping will simply share the proceeds with those who've gone on to other lives).

But, regardless of advancing age, the future for many growers still is immediate, rather than long-term. "I work for a bunch of optimistic guys," said Borck. "Next year will always be better. 'I'm going to plant, and the rains will come at the right time, and next year's crop' . . . they have to be optimistic. My growers would tell you, twenty years from now we'll still be farming. What they'll be doing, I'm not too sure. I hope that they're farming wheat. But what will the farms look like? Boy, I don't have a glass ball. I really think that we will be importing more food from overseas. I think the farms that we have, we will be farming for the environment and conservation, carbon sequestration, wind, it'll be a different farm than we are used to today. And there will be a lot more land in grass."

Roger Krug also sees change ahead for Adams County's dryland farms, but his views diverge. "I don't think it's going to be greener. Land's going to be in production. Certainly there will be always some Conservation Reserve Program, because it's good for the environment, plus they're going to be selling carbon credits on that stuff to the oil companies, that kind of thing going on. But I don't think it's going so much to grass. There's going to be as much land in production, it's just going to be different crops. Everybody agrees that there's not going to be as much wheat. But the land's going to be in production. It'll be in crop in renewable resources, cellulose, oil crops, alcohol. We're going to be making our own fuel crops, and we can do it."

Krug continues: "You've got to be an optimist. If you're not an optimist, you won't be a farmer. You either go out of business or you'll have nightmares. Because it is the ultimate gamble, take all your money and put it out in the field, and hope that the rain comes at the right time, no damage from frost. They're going to pay guys not to farm, but the bio-renewables are going to put them back in action. You've got to think outside the parameters. Guys who think inside the box are going to be the first guys gone."

In the context of current world trends, Krug has good evidence for his contention. Farmers such as Grant Miller already are shifting part of their crop from export white wheat to the red varieties more in demand for domestic use.[3]

But Krug's optimism jumps beyond such realism, definitely going outside the box. He foresees future demand for agri-tourism, for instance, "like they're doing right now out near Othello, charging people good money to round up their cows. Run the cows down to where there's a chuckwagon, and have a chuckwagon dinner, that kind of stuff." And his visions really leave the box entirely behind when it comes to fuel crops—not just growing them, but using them too. "Switchgrass, you can get eight to nine ton per acre, and you know, if you've got forty ton, you can run a one megawatt power plant that'll give you power for a thousand homes. So you may see a power plant in Washtucna, one in Ritzville, gasifying silage and then generating with the gas."[4]

When it comes to the fate of the area's small towns, though, Roger shares Gretchen Borck's pessimism—if for somewhat different reasons. Borck's projection of fewer active farms, whether through idling the land for conservation or because a farm family just quits, means the local civic structure will take even more hits. "Absolutely, yes. There will be a ripple effect definitely, not only for the economy, but for the schools, for the county taxes, health services, education, all the way around the block, everything will be affected by it."

Krug also sees a future of fewer farms, albeit more of them producing crops than the Wheat Growers' Issues Director predicts. But he shares Borck's pessimism regarding the future of dryland settlements, albeit for a different reason. "Towns that have economic development programs, or are successful at marketing themselves," says Krug, "they'll still be here. The towns that can't will continue to decay and die."

Othello, of course, is a star in this category, but a star in an otherwise dimming Adams County firmament. Benge, Cunningham, Hatton, Ralston, all moribund. Washtucna too, unless Krug's imagined power plant pops up there. Tokio, all but nonexistent, will surely see commercial resurgence if the proposed Burlington Northern cargo trailer terminal locates there, let alone the possible ethanol plant. But residential increase from Tokio-area ventures likely will benefit Ritzville, just ten miles away, which may thereby find a way to expand beyond its current, shrunken economic boundaries of elevators, limited retail, bars, movies, and, of course county government. Lind has a chance, says Krug. He refers cautiously to the latest in that city's hopes that some New Age light industry—electronics assembly or some such—may take advantage of the new well, and the streets and sidewalks refurbished by state grants.

In the wet western end of the county, Othello flourishes in conjunction with the food processing industry. A goodly portion of the potatoes processed there and in nearby Warden are grown on land irrigated by the existing Columbia Basin Project canals. But another goodly portion is grown on fields watered by groundwater wells. What happens to that portion of the crop if their wells go dry before the new Basin Project water comes in?

Dale Lathim, Executive Director of the Potato Growers of Washington, is confident that any displaced spuds, the highest value crop, will find new sprinkled ground—by displacing other irrigated crops on land already watered by the existing canals. If he's right, it's only the anti-obesity folks who pose any threat to the tuber sector of local growing and processing.

But that's at best a questionable optimism. As the study cited in chapter 11 pointed out, a serious cutback in pumped irrigation in Adams County before the new Grand Coulee water arrives will have painful, rippling impact on the local economy: harvesting, trucking, processing, you name it.

That disruption would be felt, though, mainly in the wet western end of the county, where the growing population of Latino immigrants already is propelling forward a cultural and socioeconomic shift. The dependence of wage labor concentrating there on irrigated farm work and its resultant food processing will be seriously undercut if the groundwater dries up.

In the drylands out east, the pains of shrinkage, unrelated to water questions, have settled in slowly and gradually over the years. The decrease in farming families and the withering of retail and other amenities has bred a kind of wary acceptance, an adjustment to diminished prospects of development. But there's still a wish to try because, most importantly, the conviction still prevails—with or without new economic inputs—that a farm-based community will be ongoing.

Lind and Ritzville yearn for the possibility that in the evolving age of global communications, remote call center operations will begin to see their way to eastern Washington as well as India. And in 2007, a first-time countywide task force of representatives from local governments and Chambers of Commerce formed to promote business development. But outside Othello, prospects are dicey, and hopes are not encouraged by two factors mentioned by Gretchen Borck. One is the steep depletion of local tax revenues, shrunken by declining population and mercantile closures, funds now insufficient to sustain more than moderate municipal services. And beyond the civic embarrassment of minimal retail establishments is the shrinkage of school-age population to the point where towns must share their facilities. The quality of educational offerings may not suffer, but the locational disjunction is hardly an enticement for the young families needed by these places where the long-term residents are aging and dying.

Hyphenated schools—Lind-Ritzville, for instance—have become the norm in the Basin's dryland regions, particularly at the high school level: Lind-Ritzville's sports teams, competing as the Broncos in the State's "B" league, find most of their opponents also in that combined category—the Wilbur-Creston Wildcats, for instance, Lacrosse-Washtucna Tigercats, even the three-town Elmira-Coulee-Hartline Warriors. And for the hyphenated towns in these arrangements, the diminution to joint status reflects erosion of one of the hallmarks of civic identity and esteem. As one parent told me, it used to be that when your high school team was playing at home, the town shut down, you couldn't even buy gas. Nowadays, there's excitement still—whole pages of photographic reportage of games, including girls' competition, in the *Ritzville-Adams County Journal*, for instance. But the civic oomph for towns that have long celebrated their prideful individuality is definitely diminished.

Even though the eastward spread of Hispanic arrivals within the county has begun to register in Lind-Ritzville and nearby student rosters, the enrollment numbers are not climbing to the level of municipal independence. As ownership of farmland consolidates, and equipment prices rise, there's literally no way for wage-earning newcomers to buy the spread needed for a sup-

portive summer fallow farm (let alone sprinkler-equipped irrigated land). And so long as dry wheat is grown on Adams's rolling loess soils, it seems that the need for wide acreage under
family control will be the operative mode—familial partnerships
and home-based corporations. There really isn't any way that
outside corporate ownership could make these dryland farms
work. The success of the farming here absolutely depends on
resident growers' intimate understanding of just what treatment the quirky needs of their dry ground has to have, field by
field, in order to be productive.

The children of dryland farmers face a similar difficulty as
regards their own hopes for farmsteads. Unless there is enough
land in the family's holdings—or enough in the family treasury
to buy more—if they want to return to become growers on their
own, they may be out of luck until their parents retire or die.
Some of these kids will, of course, head elsewhere for nonfarm
lives. But some will become farm support workers, everything
from agronomists to delivering fuel and chemicals.

Those who do return to work the family land, however, face
the social difficulties that accompany the disappearance of town
amenities that their parents relied on. Of the three children of
Grant and Nancy Miller, Amy, the oldest, taking a degree in
agronomics, may follow a career in agribusiness. Karlee, the
youngest, just beginning college, has not yet decided. But Matt,
middle child, who'll graduate from Washington State University, wants nothing more than to farm with his father, and certainly will do that until—and after—Grant retires.

Matt's mother, Nancy, who in marrying Grant had to weather
the change from town living to the remoteness of the Miller
homestead out south of Lind, sees a harder future for her son.
"As a mother I really worry about Matthew coming home to
farm. In Lind, the churches are closing, everything's closing. So

how is he and his family—what is that going to look like? If he lives here, then you're going to—what? The kids are going to go to school in Ritzville and you're here? The whole picture, I really worry about isolation."

But it's an isolation that many noise- and crime-bedevilled urban dwellers could only wish for. Within this dispersion there are currents of connection that sustain a fellowship of common endeavor, a connection that continues out in the dryland even among those who have to drive ten, fifteen miles to get the mail, or even to see their neighbors' faces. Take a composite picture of the many events in 2006 that brought together this dispersed community in either mutual endeavor or mutual enjoyment. Hold the shot. It shows a network of supportive relationships by which a functioning rural society sustains itself. And in a nation increasingly captive to the blandishments of individualizing electronic whiz-bang, it continues as a wistful reminder of what we used to like best about ourselves.

When Lind-area wheat grower Michael Connor died of a heart attack in August of 2006, his fields were ready to cut. As reported by the *Ritzville-Adams County Journal*'s Jennifer Larsen, "At least a dozen area farmers offered equipment." Friend and neighbor Rubben Labes, who organized the bee, had to refuse offers of equipment from "at least a dozen" other farmers because there were already enough. "They would've been running over each other out there," he said.

"Grant Miller was unavailable for the Bee day, but had cut 175 acres in the previous week," reported Larsen. "People started their way toward the Conner farm as early as 3:30 AM. At least fifty were there for breakfast at 7:00 AM on the lawn. There were a John Deere, a Gleaner, and three Case International combines, two tractor-bankout wagon combos, and five trucks including two semis. Plus three fire trucks, a precaution the department provides for harvesting events that put a lot of machinery in one field."

The volunteer crew harvested until 4:00 PM, then had dinner on the lawn, food prepared by Michael's widow, Tina, with help from Rubben's sister, Mickie Stanley. The last helpers left at 9:00 PM. "It was a good day, It was a sad day, but it was a good day," said Tina, who had only moved with their daughters to the farm six years before. "I've never been a part of something so huge. I've never lived in a community that's done that."

Change, always coming, may shrink or damage the continuity of the dryland's admirable neighborly support network. But at least in the near future the past will cling. There will still be the Wheatlands Fair in Ritzville, showcasing prizewinning flowers and garden produce, right along with the 4-H kids' cattle, rabbits, chickens, pigs and sheep. Plus the rodeo, celebrating the stock-raising tradition of Jake Harder and his fellow ranchers. There will be harvest celebrations for the wheat crop, too, although the rowdiness that these used to bring is gone, along with the old-time presence of migrant crews.

For the time being, each new year will bring Lind's Demolition Derby, featuring parade and picnic. Harvest dances. Fourth of July celebrations around the county featuring slow cavalcades of historic vehicles and floats from all over the western side of the Columbia Basin, gorgeously caparisoned floats that present each town's princesses to the larger world.

Don't let the image fade. Change will continue, but for the moment in this long, evolving reach of time, this is Adams County as it has become. As it is becoming.

Notes

Prelude: Noah's Gift

1. Clifford E. Trafzer and Richard D. Scheuerman, *Chief Joseph's Allies* (Newcastle, Calif.: Sierra Oaks Publishing Company, 1992), condensed from quotations on 7–8.

Chapter Two: The Mixed Blessing of Roads

1. *Ritzville-Adams County Journal*, Centennial Edition, December 1983, p. 59.
2. Ruth Kirk and Carmela Alexander, *Exploring Washington's Past, A Road Guide to History* (Seattle: University of Washington Press, 1990), 208.
3. Ibid.

Chapter Five: Tenacity

1. *Ritzville-Adams County Journal*, Centennial Edition, December 1983, p. 33.
2. Ibid.
3. *The History of Adams County* (Ritzville, Wash.: Adams County Historical Society, 1986), 252.
4. This is gawky but effective equipment, motorized long trains of wheeled, connected sprinkler pipe that slowly track around a well head, watering usually 125 acres. The result yields real crop circles, not those supposedly created by visitors from outer space.

They're visible even from commercial airliners flying high overhead. There's more on this technology and its consequences in chapters 9 and 11.

5. See more on the perilous vagaries of potato marketing in chapter 9.

Chapter Six: They Feed in the Coulees

Epigraph: Some interpretations of this song hold that the correct version, which indeed is the way it's usually sung, is *"the* fiery and snuffy *are* rarin' to go," and that *fiery* refers to a paint (*i.e.,* multicolored) horse and *snuffy* is a buff (*i.e.,* snuff-) colored animal. This conjecture gains credence (or perhaps takes invention?) from the first line of the song: "I ride an old paint, I lead an old dan, I'm gone to Montana. . . ." Yet another exegesis asserts that *fiery* and *snuffy* were the nicknames of railroad engines that conveyed cattle from a certain area to market. Since it's known that one way cowboys calmed their herds was to ride around them singing, I've chosen the version presented here as making the most sense.

1. Alexander Campbell McGregor, *Counting Sheep: From Open Range to Agribusiness on the Columbia Plateau* (Seattle: University of Washington Press, 1982), 19, 29 ff.

2. "Mars Rover," NASA web site. Press release, Public Information Office, Jet Propulsion Laboratory, California Institute of Technology, National Aeronautics and Space Administration, Pasadena, Calif., June 19, 1997.

Chapter Nine: In the Land of the Potato

Epigraph: Milton Meltzer, *The Amazing Potato* (New York: HarperCollins, 1992), jacket blurb.

1. Gertrude Stein, *Everybody's Autobiography* (New York: Random House, 1937), 298.

2. *Potato Grower Magazine,* vol. 31, no. 10 (October 2003).

Chapter Ten: The Fruitful Descendants of Ammann, Hutter, and Menno

1. These figures are from Laura Wilson, *Hutterites of Montana* (New Haven, Conn.: Yale University Press, 2000), 12.

2. In John Sayles's film *Matewan*, a United Mineworkers' labor organizer who had been imprisoned at the same time for his pacifism belittles his own bravery in comparison to those brothers. The film identifies them as Mennonites, but they were Hutterites.

3. Neighbors often grouse that the Hutterite colonies get special tax exemption as church bodies. Not true. They pay local and state taxes the same as other property holders. And the Internal Revenue Service levies on them as corporations, in the category of Communal Religious Communities, under section 501D of the IRS code. It's just that with collective ownership of the corporate assets, the taxable amount assigned to each member results in a lesser assessed payment than if the whole bill were assigned to single corporate entity.

Chapter Eleven: Vanishing Lifeblood

1. The United States Bureau of Reclamation, announcing a study of one major sector of the Basin's groundwater, put it this way: "The aquifer is declining to such an extent that the ability of farmers to irrigate their crops is at risk and domestic, commercial, municipal, and industrial uses and water quality are also affected."

2. Adams County commissioner Rudy Plager asserted that "The impact to the communities is really not addressed. . . . [The study] really doesn't hit on the human loss." *Ritzville-Adams County Journal*, December 27, 2007.

3. But some of the interbeds dive too low either for recharge or for artesian pressure to be a useful factor. Their contents—water which pooled a million years ago at what became great depth, ancient water that has stewed there in the heat from the earth's core, absorbing chemicals from the rock in which it's cooked—that's the stuff that can't be used. Effectively, it's the bottom.

Epilogue

1. One theory is that molecules of water—and there had to be a big bunch of them—came in from comets and other celestial bodies that collided with Earth in its formative stages. How did water's atomic combinations emerge during the Big Bang that produced all that galactic detritus? It's an unsolved quandary that gives background to space scientists' consuming quest to find evidence of the liquid on other planets and their satellites.

2. But a hydrogen-fueled engine, which combines that gas with oxygen for combustion, does produce water as exhaust.

3. Just to prove that predicting farm futures is a chancy business, the 2007 crop year, plagued by drought in Australia and China, pushed the price for white wheat up to an unheard of $10.00 per bushel. No one believes that will last, and after all, next year the Adams crop could crash. But, in the meantime, there was joy in wheat country.

4. Even further beyond Krug's box is the emerging science of carbon sequestration—capturing the greenhouse gas carbon dioxide from power plants and such, and pumping it down it down old wells into the basalt, where chemical interaction will convert it to calcium carbonate-clamshell material. But this technology is in earliest days.

Bibliography

Allen, John Eliot, and Marjorie Burns, with Sam C. Sargent. *Cataclysms on the Columbia*. Portland, Ore.: Timber Press, 1986.

Alt, David D., and Donald W. Hyndman. *Roadside Geology of Washington*. Missoula, Mont.: Mountain Press Publishing Co., 1984.

Alwin, John A. *Between the Mountains: A Portrait of Eastern Washington*. Northwest Geographer series, no. 1. Bozeman, Mont.: Northwest Panorama Publishing, 1984.

Anglin, Ron. *Forgotten Trails: Historical Sources of the Columbia's Big Bend Country*. Edited by Glen W. Lindeman. Pullman: Washington State University Press, 1995.

Brumfield, Kirby. *This Was Wheat Farming*. Atglen, Pa.: Schiffer Publishing, Ltd. 1997.

Daniels, Dr. Catherine H. *Sustainable Agriculture in Washington State*. Pullman, Wash.: Washington State University Press, 2002.

Davis, Sharon P., ed. and contributing writer. *From Wheat to Flour*. Washington, D.C.: Millers' National Federation, and Englewood, Colo.: Wheat Foods Council, 1996.

Eastwood, Harland. *Ritzville Trading Company 1904–1968*. Published by author, 2004.

From Sagebrush to Satellite: Facts and Folklore about Lind, Washington, 1888–1988. Lind Centennial Publication Committee, 1988.

Galbraith, Jean (Oestreich), and Joan (Oestreich) Schwisow. *Our Volga German Heritage*. Published by the authors, 1988.

Gleick, Peter H., et al. *The World's Water 1998–1999*, et seq. Pacific Institute for Studies in Development, Environment, and Security. Washington, D.C.: Island Press.

Granatstein, David. *Amber Waves: A Sourcebook for Sustainable Dryland Farming in the Northwestern United States.* Seattle: Washington State University Press, 1992.

Hein, Teri. *Atomic Farmgirl: The Betrayal of Chief Qualchan, the Appaloosa, and Me.* Golden, Colo.: Fulcrum Publishing, 2000.

The History of Adams County Washington. Adams County Historical Society, 1986.

Hostetler, John A., and Gertrude Enders Huntington. *The Hutterites in North America.* New York: Holt, Rinehart and Winston, 1967.

Kirk, Ruth, and Carmela Alexander. *Exploring Washington's Past: A Road Guide to History.* Seattle: University of Washington Press, 1990.

Lange, Ian M. *Ice Age Mammals of North America: A Guide to the Big, the Hairy, and the Bizarre.* Missoula, Mont.: Mountain Press Publishing Co., 2002.

McGregor, Alexander Campbell. *Counting Sheep: From Open Range to Agribusiness on the Columbia Plateau.* Seattle: University of Washington Press, 1982.

Managing Water in the West: Odessa Subarea Special Study, Columbia Basin Project. Ellen Berggren, study manager. Washington, D.C.: U.S. Bureau of Reclamation, 2006.

Meltzer, Milton. *The Amazing Potato.* New York: HarperCollins, 1992.

Menno Mennonite Church Centennial History Book, 1900–2000. Menno, Wash.: Menno Centennial Celebration Committee, Bill Dyck, chairman.

O'Garro, Mary Ann. *Profiles of Daily Living: Adams, Grant and Lincoln Counties.*

Mary Ann O'Garro, analyst. Grant County Health District, 2002.

Reisner, Marc, and Sarah Bates. *Overtapped Oasis: Reform or Revolution for Western Water.* Washington, D.C.: Island Press, 1990.

Ritzville-Adams County Journal. Centennial Edition, 1983.

Trafzer, Clifford E., and Richard D. Scheuerman. *Chief Joseph's Allies.* Newcastle, Calif.: Sierra Oaks Publishing Company, 1992.

Wilson, Laura. *Hutterites of Montana.* New Haven: Yale University Press, 2000.